Praise for
140 Twitter Tips for Educators

"*140 Twitter Tips for Educators* is the perfect PD for those who don't get Twitter in education. You'll unleash learning and get excited about teaching again, 140 characters at a time. #awesome."

—**Vicki Davis** (@coolcatteacher)
Mashable "Rockstar" Teacher on Twitter,
host of "Every Classroom Matters,"
author of The Cool Cat Teacher blog
and *Reinventing Writing*

"Being 'unconnected' is no longer a choice in the field of education. *140 Twitter Tips for Educators* calms your every fear about embracing Twitter, and provides you with the knowledge to advance your students' lives, as well as your career, to heights you never dreamed of!"

—**Glenn Robbins** (@glennr1809)
2016 NASSP Digital Principal of the Year,
Middle School Principal, Northfield, New Jersey

"Twitter is a tool that educators can use to connect globally and build their PLNs (Personal/Professional Learning Networks). In this book, Brad, Billy, and Scott give 140 practical tips that educators can use to leverage the power of social media to help their pedagogy. Readers will glean chunks of wisdom from the Twitter experts who brought us #Satchat and inspired thousands of educators worldwide."

—**Sarah Thomas** (@sarahdateechur)
Digital Innovation in Learning Award Winner,
Regional Technology Coordinator,
Prince George's County, Maryland

"Currie, Krakower and Rocco provide something for everyone with their great new book *140 Twitter Tips for Educators*. From the novice twitter user, to the seasoned social media professional, anyone can find rich tidbits on how to get the most out of a personalized, professional learning network. Their collective leadership in the Twittersphere not only positively influences the lives of individual educators, but strengthens the American education system as a whole."

—**Winston Sakurai** (@winstonsakurai)
2016 NASSP Digital Principal of the Year,
Upper School Principal, Mililani, Hawaii

"Technology in education isn't going away anytime soon, but it is constantly changing. *140 Twitter Tips for Educators* illustrates how all educators, whether they are connected or not, can use Twitter to help them grow professionally and improve their instructional practices. This book is filled with easy to follow strategies to use Twitter: from branding and marketing your school and classroom to becoming an advocate for the education field using Twitter, this book has it all. As a fellow connected educator, I learned additional ways to use Twitter to help my staff and myself grow. I would encourage anyone who is looking to get better as an educator to read this book."

—**Bobby Dodd** (@bobby_dodd)
2016 NASSP Digital Principal of the Year,
Principal, Gahanna, Ohio

To the educators in our Twitter family: You inspire us to be innovative and do what's best for kids. Thank you.

*This book is dedicated to my wife Leigh, son Cooper, daughter Sydney, mother Karen, and father Bruce. Thank you for always believing in me and supporting my efforts over the years. A special shout-out to Scott Rocco and Billy Krakower. We were put on this earth to collaborate and change the face of education.—**Brad Currie***

*This book is dedicated to my daughter Brianna, who is too young right now to realize that her dad is up at seven thirty on a Saturday morning to talk to educators and not change her dirty diapers. To my wife Jennifer, who allows me to spend an hour on a Saturday talking with other educators as she takes care of our daughter. To my parents, for always believing in me and supporting my efforts over the years.—**Billy Krakower***

This book is dedicated to my family who always questioned why anyone would ever want to get up at seven thirty in the morning on Saturdays to Tweet with me about school, education, and learning. I told you someone was interested!

*To my wife, Tracy, who has always taken care of the family while I continue to explore the world of social media. And to my kids, Paige, Nicholas, and Michael, who find I get nerdier as I learn online and are not afraid to tell me when I get too into this stuff.—**Scott Rocco***

140 Twitter Tips for Educators

by Brad Currie, Billy Krakower, and Scott Rocco, EdD

©2016 by Evolving Educators

Published by Dave Burgess Consulting, Inc.
San Diego, CA

http://daveburgessconsulting.com

Cover Design by Genesis Kohler
Interior Design by My Writers' Connection

Library of Congress Control Number: 2016934319
Paperback: ISBN: 978-0-9861555-8-1
Ebook: ISBN: 978-0-9861555-9-8

First Printing: March 2016

140 Twitter Tips for Educators

by Brad Currie, Billy Krakower,
and Scott Rocco, EdD

#Contents

Introduction

"Why Twitter?
It flattens titles in the educational world and provides a family atmosphere full of sharing and collaboration."
—@bradmcurrie

Welcome to *140 Twitter Tips for Educators.* This book is a product of our passion for and the belief all three of us have in Twitter and the effect it can have in the lives of educators from all walks of life. Twitter offers something for everyone. Are you a teacher looking for an engaging lesson idea? How about a school principal searching for ideas to improve school culture? A superintendent wanting to inform stakeholders of district happenings? Whatever questions you have about education or about how you can be even better at your job, you'll find ideas, resources, and a vibrant network of professionals ready to help you on Twitter. It's your one-stop shopping experience for all things education, and it provides a venue to share best practices in order to promote the success of students.

During the past five years, Twitter has been an integral part of our professional and personal lives. In fact, the three of us would have never met, became great friends, started #Satchat, presented at conferences, formed Evolving Educators, LLC, or written this book if it were not for Twitter. More importantly, our lives as educators might have remained status quo if it were not for the sharing of ideas and resources by educators from all over the world on Twitter. There is no better place than Twitter to share, connect, collaborate, reflect, and ultimately improve your practice as an educator. We hope that you enjoy reading this book. More importantly, we hope you will use at least a few of these ideas to better yourself, your students, your school, your district, and your community. You can read this book in one shot, in small chunks, or when a situation presents itself. Sit back, relax, and enjoy your ride on the Twitter spaceship.

This book is formatted in three sections based on your experience and comfort level with Twitter as a tool for education. Each section builds upon the last, but also provides you the opportunity to use any of the items or sections independently, based on your existing experience and comfort level with Twitter. You will quickly discover that the simple concept of a 140-character message has a tremendous amount of potential and Twitter is actually a rather robust system with near limitless potential for educators.

Section I is all about **getting started**. This section is for educators not currently on Twitter, who have a minimal working knowledge of the social media platform uses for educational purposes, or who want to learn more about its features and what other educators are doing. You will learn how to open a Twitter account, build a great profile, and develop a personal learning network (PLN). In short, you'll discover the basics that every educator should know about Twitter.

Section II focuses on **taking Twitter to a higher level**. Here, you will go from a basic understanding of how to use Twitter in education to becoming an active participant and contributor, so you can add to the flow of information Tweeted and consumed.

Section III is about **becoming a Twitter rock star**. In this section, you'll learn about features that enhance Tweets, online resources that can be used in conjunction with Twitter, and how to become a consistent provider of quality information on Twitter. In the process, you will become a connected educator whom other educators rely upon for information and support.

> *Note:* We've included screenshots of some of the tips presented in *140 Twitter Tips for Educators* to make it easy to start using Twitter immediately. The way Twitter looks can vary depending on the device or app you're using, but in almost all cases you will be able to complete the action regardless of whether you're on a desktop, laptop, tablet, or smartphone. If you don't immediately see the button or menu item we identify, be patient and explore the options available on your device. You'll very likely find the right button or link. And if you don't, send one of us a Tweet and we'll help you out!

SECTION 1
Getting Started

Welcome to the world of social media. More importantly, welcome to the world of Twitter for educators. It's fascinating to think how a little blue bird with a limited number of characters can influence so many people, particularly educators. No other resource that we have used has had such a positive and profound effect on us as educators in such a short time. The connections Twitter has empowered us to make with educators in our state, country, and around the world have opened the door to more learning and more resources than any of us could have imagined.

For Billy, Twitter has directly affected his instruction in his classroom. He has been able to bring in new ideas and concepts to his classroom—ideas he'd never thought about before becoming a connected educator. He has done Mystery Skype calls, brought in experts, and connected his classroom with other classrooms doing survey and weather studies. None of this would have been possible had Billy not joined Twitter and participated in Twitter chats.

Scott has discovered the power of Twitter for gaining access to new and valuable professional learning networks. In addition, he has connected with outstanding educators and influencers from around the globe—people with whom he never would have had an opportunity to connect were it not for Twitter. And he appreciates the opportunities that learning this relatively new medium has given him to influence others through keynote addresses and presentations at local and state conferences. From New Jersey to Alaska, Scott has been honored to discuss his passion for and belief in Twitter and social media as valuable tools for educators.

For Brad, Twitter has been a game changer, especially in the past five years. Prior to becoming a connected educator on Twitter, Brad had limited access to best practice resources and ideas that challenged his educational mindset. Today, Brad has access to Tweets shared by educators from around the world on a daily basis. He shares his own thoughts and resources pertaining to innovation in the field of education on Twitter. More importantly, though, Brad has learned to leverage the power of Twitter to help impact the success of students in his own school district.

For each of us, Twitter has become the go-to tool for connecting, collaborating, creating, learning, and reflecting with educators from all walks of life. And our hope is that this book will equip and encourage you to make the most of Twitter. Perhaps you've thought about it, researched it, maybe even talked to someone who is on it, but you haven't taken the plunge yet. It's time. Let's get you started on Twitter so you can begin using what has the potential to be one of the most important and valuable resources for your professional learning as an educator. Section I walks you through the key steps for opening an account, setting up your profile, getting your first Tweet out, and building your PLN.

Start with the Basics

#1 Do I Have to Sign Up for Twitter to Use It?

Let's start off with the most pressing question educators have about Twitter: *Do I have to sign up for Twitter to use it?*

The answer is **no!** You do not have to be a registered user to reap some of the benefits Twitter offers. One way to access a person's or organization's Twitter page is to use Google to search Twitter.

For example, to see what *Teach Like a PIRATE* author Dave Burgess is up to on Twitter, simply type in "Dave Burgess Twitter" in the search box, and many results will pop up. Then,

Figure 1-1

all you have to do is click the link and it will bring you right to his account. Take a look at the screenshot (Figure 1-1) to get an idea of what a Twitter search looks like on Google. People or places will often embed their Twitter feed on their website or blog. Check out Twitter. It can't hurt.

Even though you don't need an account to see what's on Twitter, if you want to connect with, learn from, and collaborate with connected educators from all around the world, you will need to register for and use a Twitter account.

Don't have a Twitter account? Well, let's get started.

#2 Create an Account

So you've decided to turn the page and explore the world of Twitter for educators—awesome! Social media is about connecting with others. And whether you're connecting online or in person, nothing beats a great first impression. Once you've made an impression, it's very difficult to change, especially if it is negative.

On Twitter, your first impression begins with your profile. So the first thing you'll need to do is take a few minutes and create an account or profile.

Go to Twitter.com.

Click *Sign up* (Figure 2-1).

Fill in your name and phone number or email and then create a password (Figure 2-2).

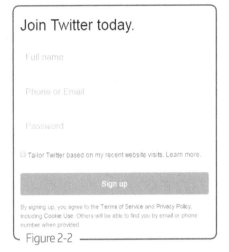

Figure 2-2

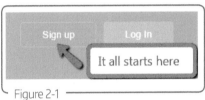

Figure 2-1

#3 Create a Twitter Handle

First name, last name, or nickname. Professional or unprofessional. *What exactly goes into creating a Twitter handle?* Frankly, it depends on what you are comfortable with using and what is available.

Some people use the first and last name, like "@bradmcurrie" (Brad M. Currie), while others use their first initial and last name, like "@wkrakower" (William [Billy] Krakower). And then some people use their first name, middle initial, and last name, like "@scottr-rocco" (Scott R. Rocco). Are you a principal? Maybe including "principal" in your Twitter handle would suit you well. Passionate about technology? Consider integrating "tech."

We each decided to use our names because they were available when we registered for our Twitter accounts. Plus, using our names makes it easy for people in school communities to find us on Twitter. Some people choose to include their titles in their Twitter handles. That's fine, but keep in mind that using a title like *teacher* or *principal* means you'll need to update your Twitter handle if you change positions. Scott and Brad included their middle initials in their handles because, believe it or not, the handles without their middle initials were already taken. You may have to try a few options until you find an available handle that is both memorable and meaningful.

#4 Personalize Your Profile

Your personal information on your Twitter profile offers the world a small glimpse into your life, is a great place to give yourself a few kudos, and helps you connect with followers based on your shared location, occupation, organization affiliations, and interests. Obviously, security and safety are paramount, so be cognizant of the information you put into cyberspace.

At the end of the day, we each have a certain comfort level with how much information is placed on our Twitter profile, so as long as you are comfortable, then that's all that matters.

Billy Krakower
@wkrakower

Author, Speaker, co-moderator of #satchat & #njed Organizer #edcampnj #edcampldr Partner @EvolvingEd LLC, ASCD Emerging Leader, Google Educator, Dad.

Scott Rocco
@ScottRRocco FOLLOWS YOU

Superintendent, TCNJ Adjunct Prof, NJEXCEL Instructor. Co-founder of #Satchat. Creator of #ASuperDay & Connect an Educator Day, Keynoter. Thoughts are mine.

Brad Currie
@bradmcurrie

Educator. #Satchat Co-Founder. #EdcampNJ Organizer. Partner @EvolvingEd LLC. @ASCD Emerging Leader. Author/Speaker. #GoogleEDU Trainer.

#5 Add a Picture and Background—No One Likes an Egg

That's right! You heard it here: No one likes an egg! In the Twitterverse, an egg as your profile photo tells a potential follower that your profile does not have much of a presence and is, therefore, a waste of time. Adding a picture and a header photo to your Twitter page gives you credibility with your potential PLN and tells the world that you really are a person. Having a face to go with your name also helps when you are at a conference and want to connect with a member of your PLN in person, but we'll get to that later.

To add a picture, log on to Twitter, click *Edit profile* on the right-hand side of the page, and click *Add your profile pic*. You will then have three options: *Upload photo*, *Take photo*, or *Remove*. If the image you want to use for your profile photo is stored on your computer, click *Upload photo* and select the desired photo. You will be given the option to adjust the image to fit Twitter's parameters. When you're satisfied, click *Apply*, and you have a profile picture.

Is a header photo necessary too? Yes! Your header photo gives potential followers a better glimpse into who you are as an educator and, more importantly, as a person. You'll notice that many well-connected educators use cover photos of them presenting at a conference, teaching a class, or simply hanging out with people they care about.

To add a header photo, the steps are very similar to those listed for adding a profile picture: Click *Change your header photo*, then upload the image, scale it to fit the space, and click *Apply*. Finally, click *Save changes* and take a look at your new page!

#6 Personalize Your Profile's Background

Figure 6-1

The first few steps in this chapter focus on setting up your Twitter account correctly so that people can easily identify who you are and what you do when they look at your profile. The next step in creating an eye-catching profile is to personalize your page's theme with a background color or an image. Your profile background is your brand, so personalize it and make it relevant to what you believe in as an educator.

Click *Settings* (Figure 6-1).

Click *Design* (Figure 6-2).

Select one of Twitter's premade themes (Figure 6-3), upload a background image, or simply change the background color to customize your page (Figure 6-4).

Design	>
Apps	>
Widgets	>
Your Twitter data	>

Figure 6-2

When you're happy with your selection, click *Save changes*.

Jennifer Hogan (@Jennifer_Hogan), a school leader from Alabama, wrote about an alternative to creating a custom background with a website called Canva. Sign up for this free tool by visiting canva.com and utilize their drag-and-drop feature and professional layouts to design stunning graphics that can be used for your Twitter page, blog, or website. Read Jennifer's blog here: http://bit.ly/1TLcqts.

Figure 6-3

Figure 6-4

#7 Follow These Eleven Educators

Your profile, profile photo, header photo, and page's theme are ready, so now let's start building your PLN by following a few people.

One of the best things about Twitter is that you can gain access to thousands of educators from around the world. By "following" people, their Tweets—ideas, best practices, comments, and questions—will show up in your Twitter feed any time you log in to the platform. So when you're deciding whom to follow, search for people who share your interests or can speak to topics you're excited about. For example, if you are a district school leader, then you might follow someone like Scott Rocco (@scottrrocco), a superintendent who has worked to expand the use of educational technology and social media in education, an adjunct professor, and a conference and keynote speaker. If you're a classroom teacher, you may want to follow Billy Krakower (@wkrakower). And building-level administrators or technology educators might follow Brad Currie (@bradmcurrie). There is someone out there for everybody. In Figure 7-1, you'll see a few of the educators we recommend following.

So how exactly do you follow someone? If you know the person's Twitter handle or name, type it into the search box at the top of the page. When you see the person you're looking for, click on their name to bring up their profile page. Following that person is as simple as clicking *Follow*. Check out the list below to see a few Twitter peeps we think every educator should follow.

Click on *Follow* and you will see the message: You are now following this person on Twitter.

Looking for more people to follow? Check out CybraryMan. com and visit the "My PLN Stars" section for a subject-specific list of educators (cybraryman.com/plnstars.html).

Figure 7-1

#8 Follow an Organization

In addition to following individual educators, you can follow educational organizations. Following professional organizations is an excellent way to expand your knowledge base and learn more about education. Start by asking yourself these questions:

- What subject/grade do I teach?

Figure 8-1

- Are there organizations associated with my grade level and subject?
- What am I interested in?
- Are there other organizations that will expand my PLN?
- What organizations am I a member of?

Your answers to these questions can help determine which groups to look up and follow.

Almost every organization has a Twitter handle, and they often share information. Figure 8-1 has three of our favorites.

#9 Know the Difference between "@" and "#"

People ask us all the time what the difference is between a Twitter handle and a hashtag. Simply put, a Twitter handle is associated with the Twitter profile and name of a person, business, or organization and is always preceded by an *at* symbol, "@." For example, @Burgess_Shelley is our friend and fellow educator Shelley Burgess.

A hashtag, on the other hand, always uses the *pound* or *number* symbol, "#," before a word, acronym, or phrase. Hashtags work like a magnet to organize, archive, and find Tweets related to a specific person, place, or thing on most social media platforms.

Take a look at Figure 9-1 to gain a clearer understanding of the difference between a hashtag and a handle. #Satchat stands for Saturday morning chat. It takes place every Saturday morning at 7:30 (ET) on Twitter. The topic for this particular Twitter chat is the importance of professional networking for educators. Stephanie Jacobs (@MsClassNSession) was our guest moderator during a previous #Satchat conversation.

Figure 9-1

#10 Understand the Language of Twitter

Twitter is an amazing tool that allows you to make a point, share a thought, or ask a question in 140 characters or less. Technically, it's microblogging and in a world that bombards us with too much information, too frequently, Twitter cuts to the chase, gets to the point, and removes irrelevant information. Now, that's awesome!

With a maximum of 140 characters, abbreviation is the norm for Tweets, as are hashtags (words or phrases preceded by a #), and links. Most Tweets from educational leaders are well-scripted, which makes them useful. When crafting your own Tweets to communicate thoughts or share resources, you may want to use these techniques. Just remember that the more symbols you put in a Tweet, the more likely it is to confuse people than interest them—so use Twitter speak wisely. Let's break down Scott's Tweet below (Figure 10-1).

Figure 10-1

The Tweet starts with Powerful! This catches the reader's attention and gently nudges him to read the rest of the Tweet. Next is the Google hashtag, #Google, which helps Scott's Tweet gain exposure when people search for Tweets relevant to Google. Scott uses more hashtags throughout his Tweet to put focus on Google Apps for Education, #GAFE, and Chromebooks, #Chromebooks. Both are huge in the educational world right now and will garner more attention for Scott's Tweet. The next part includes a shortened link to a blog post on the subject, providing the reader a direct link to a resource, rather than a simple mention—something Twitter users appreciate. The last part of the Tweet credits the blog post's author, @EdTech_12. This is part of Twitter etiquette and a sound practice in the virtual world.

#11 More Twitter Lingo

Retweet

A Retweet is when you share a Tweet that you find interesting with your followers. Be sure to put "RT" in front of the Tweet so people know you have Retweeted someone else's work.

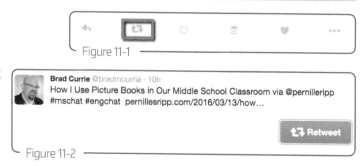

Figure 11-1

Figure 11-2

Simply click on the Retweet symbol (in the red box in Figure 11-1), and you will see the option to Retweet what someone has already Tweeted. Even as Twitter has updated how you can Retweet and what it looks like in your Twitter feed, it's important to use the RT to signal a Retweet of someone else's Tweet.

Press the Retweet button and that Tweet is now Retweeted (Figure 11-2).

Comment

A comment is when you Retweet some-one's Tweet and add words to your Retweet. You could post a comment to alert your followers to something interesting, when you want to share the Tweet using a hashtag, or if you just want to comment on a Retweet.

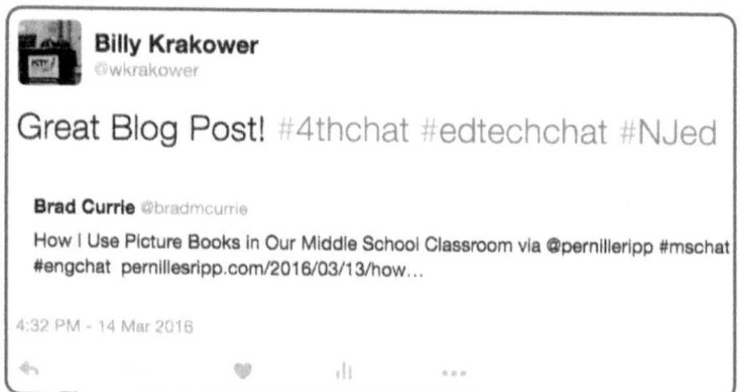

Click on *Add Comment* (Figure 11-3) and type your comment in the message box. Your comment will appear above the Tweet you're referencing (Figure 11-4).

Figure 11-3

Figure 11-4

Modified Tweet

You create a modified Tweet ("MT") when you copy and paste someone's Tweet and change it in some way, shape, or form. As long as you indicate that you've modified the Tweet by putting "MT" in front of it and give credit where credit is due by including the user's Twitter handle, then a modified Tweet is perfectly acceptable. Twitter recently came out with an update that allows you to comment on a Tweet without the original Tweet counting against your 140 characters. But if you ever change the content of someone else's Tweet, it is good Twitter etiquette to include the MT.

#12 Be Brief

One of the most beloved and hated parts of Twitter is the fact that you have 140 characters to convey a complete thought. If you love this, you understand that those 140 characters are not a limitation and can actually open up a new world for educators. If you hate it, you will struggle with getting information out. Over time, you will adjust—and may even start forming Tweets in your head throughout the day.

We live in the "now generation." We want information immediately and don't want to spend a tremendous amount of time reading, so the 140-character limitation fits our culture perfectly. However, you can extend your Tweet's 140 characters and make brevity a learning experience by including a picture, document, or form; linking to a website or article; posting a poll; asking a question; or starting a hashtag.

Your First Tweet

#13 Read Before You Tweet and Retweet

Before you Tweet or Retweet (share someone else's Tweet) for the first time, follow this one Golden Rule:

Read what you Tweet or Retweet before you post it.

Why? Because you are building a personal brand and reputation as a connected educator. You'll want to check your Tweets for the same reason you'd ask your students to proofread their work. Typos and mistakes don't look good in homework—or in Tweets.

The Retweet button is a valuable Twitter tool that allows you to share someone else's Tweet with all of your followers at once. But before you click to Retweet, double-check the post—and any links it contains—for sentences, images, emojis, or phrases that don't jive with your way of thinking or that may offend your followers. Don't assume something is kosher without looking at exactly what the Tweet says, even if it's from a good friend or colleague.

Remember: you are creating a digital résumé and brand for yourself through Twitter. It only takes a minute or so to proofread your Tweet and to scan others' Tweets before Retweeting. The majority of the time, the Tweet will be perfectly fine, but that one time it isn't—well, we won't talk about that!

#14 When Is the Best Time to Tweet?

"When should I Tweet?" "When will the most people see my Tweet for maximum exposure?" People ask us these questions all the time. Our answer is this: Don't get hung up on times. When you have time, Tweet. Good Tweets, ones that add to the educational conversation and that people find interesting, will be favorited and Retweeted.

Tweet when you are at a conference, when you see something that you want to let others know about, or when you find something your followers would be interested in. When you see your students or a colleague doing something great, Tweet about it. When you learn something that would be useful for others to know, share it in a Tweet. We have Tweeted very early in the morning, throughout our day, and even late in the evening.

The theme here is that the optimal time to Tweet is less about the hour of the day and more about what is going on around you and your Tweet's content. And as you become a consistent Tweeter, you will start to see this. It's more important to actually Tweet and to Tweet consistently than it is to worry about what time of day you Tweet. (We will get to building your Twitter stamina later in the book.)

#15 Be Retweetable

Try not to use all 140 characters in a Tweet. That's right. You read that correctly. "Why?" you may ask. For the simple fact that staying under 140 characters helps your followers Retweet your Tweet. We recommend that you leave between eight and fifteen characters in your Tweet so that one of your followers or an educator in the Twittersphere can place RT (Retweet) or comment in front of your original Tweet.

In Figure 15-1 you can see that ten characters are left in case someone else wants to Retweet our Tweet in their own special way.

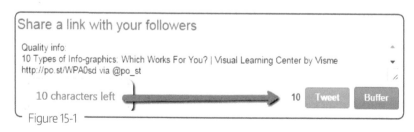

Share a link with your followers

Quality info:
10 Types of Info-graphics: Which Works For You? | Visual Learning Center by Visme
http://po.st/WPA0sd via @po_st

10 characters left ⟶ 10 Tweet Buffer

Figure 15-1

#16 It's OK If No One Notices Your First Tweet

You have an account, your profile is ready to go, and you are no longer an egg. It's time to post your first Tweet. This is one of the most nerve-racking things you will ever do on Twitter.

"What will people think?" "Will it be Retweeted?" "Will I lose my job?" In all likelihood, your first Tweet will go relatively unnoticed, but it will be part of your digital footprint and the start of your Twitter life. More importantly, and on a positive note, you are one step closer to becoming a connected educator, which can lead to some of the most exciting opportunities in your professional career.

Okay, we hear you, enough with all this fluff—let's Tweet!

#17 Compose Your First Tweet

Composing a Tweet is simple, and no matter what device you are using, the Tweet icon looks the same. Start by clicking the icon with a quill pen (Figure17-1). *Compose new Tweet* will then pop up and you can begin typing your Tweet. Remember that you have 140 characters to share your message and add links, words, and hashtags. Twitter will help you keep track of how many characters you have left. So make a statement, announce your presence on Twitter, or just Retweet someone else's Tweet.

Figure 17-1

Once you've composed your Tweet, reread it to ensure the message you want to send is what you've typed, and then click the blue *Tweet* button (Figure 17-2).

Ready? Click *Tweet*. Go ahead—it will be fine.

Now that wasn't too bad, was it?

Welcome to Twitter, and congratulations for joining the world of connected educators.

Figure 17-2

#18 Delete a Tweet

"Wait, I just sent that out to the Twitterverse?" Yes. "Can I delete it?" You sure can.

Deleting your Tweet is easy: Start by clicking the button with three dots at the bottom right side of your Tweet, and choose *Delete Tweet* from the options provided. When you do, your Tweet will pop up on the screen along with the options to *Cancel* or *Delete* (Figure 18-1). Select *Delete*, and your Tweet is gone.

Figure 18-1

Note: You can only delete your Tweet—not someone else's Tweet. And once your Tweet has been quoted by another user, it will still exist in the Twitterverse, even if you delete the original Tweet. (See #34: Block Unwanted Spam Accounts to learn how to deal with unwanted or spam Tweets.)

#19 Save a Tweet as a Draft

Sometimes you may want to compose a Tweet but wait to send it. In this case, you can save your Tweet as a draft.

Simply click *Tweet*, and your last draft message will still be there for you (Figure 19-1). If you want to save a message as a draft to send out later, we recommend that you save it in another app like Buffer (explained later in the book) and set a time for the Tweet to go out.

Figure 19-1

#20 Get Your Tweet Retweeted

As a connected educator who is looking to grow your PLN, getting a Tweet Retweeted will help you gain exposure to other connected educators who have yet to follow you. Getting your Tweet Retweeted is less about popularity and more about relevant content that others find valuable to them. There are several ways to make this happen.

First, people often search for Tweets using popular hashtags relating to a specific topic, so include hashtags like #Satchat or #tlap in the Tweet itself to help more people notice your content. However, we want to caution you on randomly using popular hashtags. Hashtags should be related to the content of the Tweet or the group of people you are trying to reach. When we Tweet and want to get information out to our PLN in New Jersey, we use #NJed. If we are looking to share with our #Satchat PLN, then the hashtag is used. You can use multiple hashtags in a Tweet; just be sure there is a purpose for their placement in your Tweet.

Another popular option is to mention people's Twitter handles to increase the odds of them noticing your Tweet and Retweeting it. Questions, catchy phrases, opinions, and sharing resources can also go a long way.

Finally, images matter. People love seeing images in their Twitter feed and are more likely to Retweet a Tweet if it has an image.

#21 Turn Motivational Tweets into Images

One of Twitter's most impressive features is the ability to be inspired by some of the best minds in education—and to inspire others. Inspirational thoughts are often Retweeted; it makes us feel good to share positive messages! If you are at a loss for things to Tweet about, scroll through your Twitter feed and look for inspirational quotes to share with your followers.

If you want to amplify a quote's power, turn it into an image using an app like InstaQuote or a website like Canva.com. Once you create your image, Tweet it by clicking on the camera icon and uploading it. You will be amazed at how frequently your inspirational images get Retweeted. Brad came across a quote from Salome Thomas-EL (@Principal_EL), an inspirational educator. Principal EL's motivational messages are always popular on Twitter. Sometimes Brad creates an image with the quote using InstaQuote and Tweets it out. Brad's followers will often Retweet these powerful images as a way to inspire *their* followers. Posting images on Twitter can make your Tweet contagious—in a good way! And when your content is shared, you build a reputation as a passionate educator (Figure 21-1).

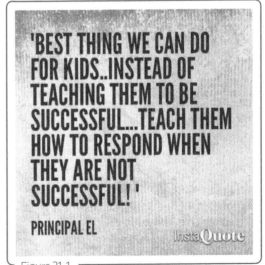

Figure 21-1

#22 Read a Book and Share Your Thoughts on Twitter

Of all the ideas we will present to you on growing your PLN and your presence on Twitter, the best are related to shared learning opportunities. Yes, you may be new to Twitter and this whole "social media thing," but you can still take advantage of the opportunities Twitter provides to learn and to share your learning with other educators. One very simple way to do that is to Tweet about the books you're reading.

Say, for example, you're reading Don Wettrick's book *Pure Genius: Building a Culture of Innovation and Taking 20% Time to the Next Level* and want to give him a shout-out on Twitter and tell others about something powerful you've read in his book. In your Tweet, include Don's Twitter handle (@DonWettrick), a few kind words, and possibly a link to his book in an online bookstore. This kind of Tweet helps build your PLN as well as your presence on Twitter. In terms of building your PLN, book recommendations are often sought after for a variety of reasons. The author will more than likely Retweet your kind shout-out, which in turns gives you more exposure on Twitter. Blasting out a Tweet like this also shows people that you are serious about professional and personal development; people with similar interests may choose to follow you for that. If the idea you share is interesting, you may get a few Retweets, which can further expand your PLN.

#23 Add a Period to Your Tweet

How could something so small be so powerful? If you wanted to reply to a Tweet or direct a Tweet to an individual or organization, you would start your Tweet with the person or organization's Twitter handle. When you add a period in front of the handle's "@," though, you send the Tweet to *everyone* you follow, allowing many more people to see it (Figure 23-1). Without the period, your Tweet only shows up in your stream, the stream of the person you Tweeted, and your shared followers' streams.

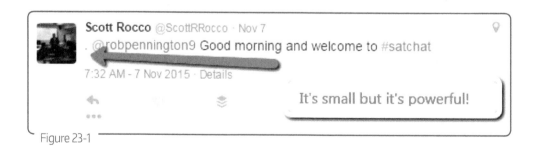

Figure 23-1

#24 Tweet Daily

To really take advantage of Twitter as a professional growth tool, consistency is key. If you are new to Twitter, try to Tweet at least once, if not twice, a day, and if you can push yourself to Tweet three times a day, that would be outstanding. Tweeting once in the morning, once in the afternoon, and once at night will increase your chances of getting your message to the masses. Over time, people will begin to notice what you are sharing and Retweet your posts to their followers.

Remember, it takes time for people to start noticing your work. But keep at it. Consistently share what you are doing in your classroom, school, or district. The more you share your best practices on Twitter and contribute to other educators' learning, the more success you, your students, school, and district will have going forward.

For now, we challenge you to commit to Tweeting at least once daily. We will delve deeper into developing a Twitter routine later.

#25 How Notifications and Mentions Can Help You Connect

Curious how you'll know one of your Tweets is recognized? Or when someone tries to connect with you by sending

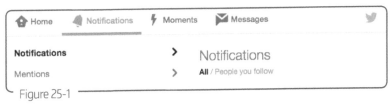

Figure 25-1

a Tweet? Every time someone Retweets your content or mentions your Twitter handle, a number will pop up on the Notifications tab in the upper left-hand corner of your Twitter page. Just click *Notifications* to find out who mentions you in a Tweet or Retweeted your content.

#26 Send a Direct Message

Twitter isn't just about sending messages out for the whole world to read. It's also about one-on-one conversations. Direct messages (DMs) allow you to send private messages to other Twitter users, without fear of your conversation ever appearing in the public Tweet stream.

To send a DM, click on the Messages icon (Figure 26-1) in your menu bar.

Figure 26-1

On a computer, you'll see a popup that says *Direct Message* and has a button for a *New message* (Figure 26-2). Click the button. If you are using a smartphone or tablet, it may look slightly different, but the concept is exactly the same.

Figure 26-2

The next screen that pops up will allow you to choose your message's recipient. Enter the person's name in the area that says *Enter a name*. **Note:** To send a DM, you must follow the person and they must be following you. As you type, names of your followers will appear. Simply select the person you want to send the DM to, and the person's name will automatically populate the line (Figure 26-3). Here, we're sending Brad a DM, and as we type his first name, his profile picture pops up.

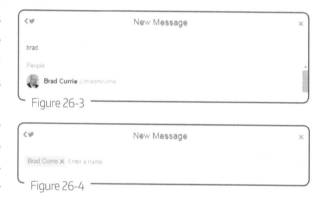

Figure 26-3

If you pick the wrong "Brad," click the X beside the name to remove it (Figure 26-4). Once you have identified the person you want to DM, click the *Next* or *Done* button in the bottom right corner.

Figure 26-4

You can now send a message, emoji, or picture (Figure 26-5). One of the best features of a DM is that you aren't limited to 140 characters.

You'll get an email or smartphone alert each time you receive a DM. If you don't want to receive those notifications, you can also turn off that feature by clicking on the three dots at the top of the message screen (Figure 26-6).

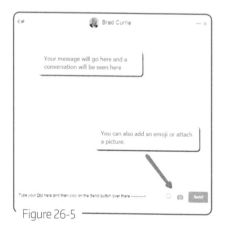

Figure 26-5

Figure 26-6

#27 Send a Group DM

If you want to share information with more than one person, you can send a group DM to a maximum of fifty Twitter users. You still have access to the features available when sending one person a DM; the only difference is that you add more names (Figure 27-1).

Just remember that the more people you add to a conversation, the more people will have access to the information you are sharing in the group DM.

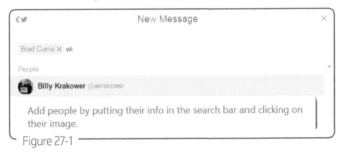

Figure 27-1

#28 To Follow ... Or Not to Follow Back

When you're new to Twitter, you're an unknown to the millions of potential followers out there. People do not know who you are or what type of content you will send out. Your profile gives them insight into what you're interested in, but savvy Twitter users also look at who you're following. That is why it's important to only follow quality people—those whom you believe will provide you equally great information.

We've already touched on how to find and follow people, which means you're already expanding your PLN. But what if the people you follow don't follow back? It happens. Don't take it personally. An unwritten Twitter rule is that you are not obligated to follow everyone back. That means not everyone you follow will follow you. That's okay!

Follow people you find interesting, people from whom you want to learn, and those with whom you want to collaborate. They may or may not feel the same way, but don't feel insulted or embarrassed—you are the only one paying attention to who is and who is not following you.

What's more, some of the people following you right now may eventually unfollow you. This is fine, too. People change who they follow all the time, and, at some point, people will find what you are Tweeting interesting and others will not. Again, this is just a natural part of participating on Twitter.

Go out and enjoy your PLN and what you are learning—your followers and sphere of influence will increase over time!

#29 Attach an Image to a Tweet

Images catch our attention. In a stream of words, a photo, drawing, or other sort of graphic stands out; attaching an image is a powerful way to enhance a Tweet.

Figure 29-1

To add an image to your Tweet from your smartphone, computer, or Google Drive, click the *Media* button below the message box (Figure 29-1).

Attach your file. Once attached, the image will appear in the bottom left side of the box. The image you see will be a thumbnail, not the full image, so don't be concerned if the image looks like a partial picture. For example, the full image in Figure 29-2 says "Evolving Educators."

If you don't like the image you've selected, click the X in the top right corner of the image box, or if you want to add another image, repeat the process. The maximum size of a photo or image is 5 MB and it must be a GIF, JPG, or PNG file. You can also add an animated GIF, but that is limited to 3 MB.

#30 Identify People in Your Image

Once you've added an image to your Tweet, a really cool thing to do is to identify who's in the photo or whom you want notified about the image. Anyone you tag in an image or Tweet will receive a notification alert about the tag.

Figure 29-2

To tag people in your photo, click *Who's in this photo?* Then begin typing the person's name or Twitter handle in the space with the magnifying glass. A list of people will appear. Select the person you want to tag. (In Figure 30-1, we've selected Scott's name.) Finally, send your Tweet.

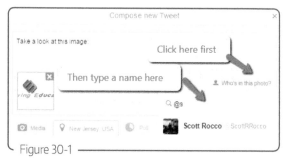

Figure 30-1

#31 Push Out Videos

In today's world, streaming video plays a large part in how we express ourselves, show what we know and have learned, and stay on top of things. Sometimes people go to sites like Twitter to find video content. For example, attendees at educational conferences often share real-time videos of the different sessions. Even if you aren't able to attend, you can still follow along by watching the posted videos. You can also share your favorite video content from other websites and apps, such as YouTube, with your followers by tapping the Twitter button on the video. You can even create and send your own videos using your smartphone or tablet. Here's how:

Figure 31-1

First, open the Twitter app on your mobile device, tap *Compose Tweet*, and then tap the camera icon in the bottom left corner (Figure 31-1).

Figure 31-3

Second, tap the blue camera icon (Figure 31-2).

Third, tap the red camera icon, record your video (Figure 31-3). Once you've captured your video, you can Tweet it to your followers

Figure 31-2

#32 Like Special Tweets to Save for Later

All three of us use Twitter for our own learning purposes and to share interesting items with our colleagues and staff members. One of the easiest ways to "save" Tweets and make them easy to find again is to "like" them and then embed into a document, almost like a monthly newsletter.

Figure 32-1

Liking a Tweet is very simple and makes it easier to find later. As a reference point, the "like" feature used to be called "favorite"

Figure 32-2

and was represented by a star. The "like" feature, referenced from this point forward, is represented by a heart. Figure 32-1 is a Tweet from Brad from our chat's archive.

The heart, highlighted with a red box, is the *like* button. The number one next to the heart indicates that one person has already liked the Tweet. You can now like it for yourself by clicking the heart (Figure 32-2), which turns the heart red and increases the number to the right.

To find that Tweet, as well as the others you've liked, click on your name to go to your personal Twitter page. You will then see a list of choices that looks like Figure 32-3.

Figure 32-3

Figure 32-4

When you click *Likes*, you will see a list of all the Tweets you've liked (Figure 32-4). You can also embed the Tweets by clicking the three little dots next to the like icon. From there it will give you a code that you can copy and paste onto your blog or website.

#33 Find and Remove Inappropriate Content

Twitter is a wonderful tool to share information, but every now and then, inappropriate content rears its ugly head. Spam Tweets can sometimes get in the way of productive sharing on Twitter.

If you find inappropriate content, you have three options:

1. Ignore it and move on.
2. Block it. (Click the three little dots at the bottom of the Tweet.)
3. Report it. (Click the three little dots for this as well.)

#34 Block and/or Report Unwanted Spam Accounts

Twitter has done a great job of controlling spam. Early on, we encountered a lot of spam. Some of it was extremely inappropriate, but there wasn't much you could do. Now, you can do a lot.

Periodically, you will see a company or a spammer sending unwanted Tweets or links. To prevent these messages from showing up in your Twitter feed, click the three dots that appear beneath every Tweet. A menu will appear and give choices about what to do with the Tweet (Figure 34-1).

Figure 34-1

If you simply want to remove a person's Tweets from your timeline, click *Mute*. If you want to restrict a user from following you, reading your Tweets, sending you a message, or tagging you in a photo, click *Block*. But if a user is abusive or spamming, read the rules about reporting violations and, if it's the best option for the situation, select *Report*. Twitter will then ask why you want to report the Tweet (Figure 34-2).

Figure 34-2

#35 How Do I Unfollow People on Twitter?

You may find that some of the educators you initially follow on Twitter ultimately don't jive with your way of thinking or, in rare instances, are inappropriate or discouraging. If the time has come to unfollow someone, simply put your cursor over the blue *Following* button until it turns red and says *Unfollow* (Figure 35-1). Click *Unfollow*, and the rest is history.

Figure 35-1

Will the person know you unfollowed them? Maybe. But unless they track who has unfollowed their Tweets using a third-party program, they initially won't. In the grand scheme of things, it shouldn't really matter whether they know or not if you believe you made the right decision.

Keep in mind that the same thing can happen to you. Don't read too much into someone unfollowing you. Aside from continuing to post meaningful content, there is really not much you can do about whether or not a person chooses to follow or unfollow you. If it really bothers you, find a way to reach out to the person to see what went wrong. In some cases, someone may have accidentally hit the wrong button and inadvertently unfollowed you.

#36 Gain Followers

There are a number of methods you can use to gain followers. Start by following other people, knowing they will more than likely follow you back. (Remember, no one is obligated to follow you back.)

Another way to gain followers is by sharing ideas. Tweet links to articles and blog posts you find interesting, share quotes, facts, or simply a note about something awesome that just happened in your school. As you consistently share relevant information and interesting ideas, more people will want to follow you.

Participating in chats is another excellent way to gain followers and expand your PLN. For example, if you participate in #Satchat every Saturday morning at 7:30 (ET), you will find a tremendous conversation going on about a relevant topic in education. Subjects range from technology integration to school culture to professional development. The more you participate in a Twitter discussion like #Satchat, the more likely you are to gain followers, especially if your message resonates with participants.

#37 Pace Yourself

Tweeting, following people, and gaining followers is fun, but there may come a point when you feel overwhelmed by the amount of information being shared. As your PLN grows, your Twitter feed will fill up with new Tweets every minute, and soon, every second. It will be impossible to read every Tweet.

Here's the good news: You don't have to keep up with all those Tweets. In fact, you're better off acknowledging from Day One that it's impossible to respond to, or even read, every Tweet.

Here's the even better news: The best and most important Tweets often come back around in the form of quotes and Retweets. Plus, you can also go back to your Tweet stream to see what you've missed or search for relevant topics and keywords using a hashtag search.

#38 Share Your Location

Sharing your location is a way to let members of your PLN see which state or country you live in. Sharing your location on Twitter is easy—and you don't have to tell people exactly where you live. When your Tweet message screen is open, you'll see the *Location* button under the typing window. Click it and your state or general region will appear in your Tweet (Figure 38-1).

Figure 38-1

#39 Change Your Tweet's Location

If you're at your school, an education conference, or on a field trip, you might want to let people know exactly where you are. You can easily change your location. Simply click *Tweet* and then click the *Location* button to choose or search for your location (Figure 39-1). Or if you *don't* want the whole world to know where you are, you can turn off your location altogether.

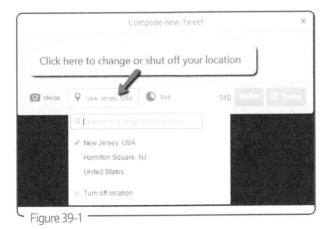

Figure 39-1

#40 Control Your Twitter Settings

To manage your settings, click on your profile picture in the top right corner of the screen and choose *Settings* from the menu. From the settings menu you'll be able to:

- Change your basic account info.
- Manage your security and privacy settings.
- Control your password.
- Manage info for your online purchases through Twitter.
- Get your in-tweet order history.
- Download Twitter's mobile app, set up your cell number, and manage the Twitter app settings on your phone.
- Control the email notifications Twitter sends you.
- Control notifications on your Twitter feed.
- Search your email's address book for people to follow.
- Mute an account and find those you've muted.
- Manage the Twitter users you have blocked.
- Change your background design.
- Manage the apps connected to your Twitter account.
- Create and manage your widgets.
- Review your account data.

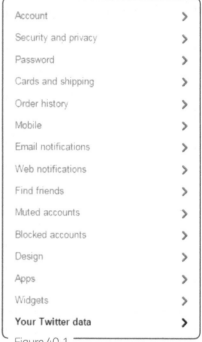

Figure 40-1

#41 Use the Search Box to Find Important Information

The search box is your friend. Really, it is! Once you've located this tool in the upper right-hand corner of your Twitter page, you'll never look back.

Looking for a hashtag? Use the search box. Having trouble finding your favorite author? Use the search box. Want to follow an educational conference virtually? Use the search box (Figure 41-1).

The search box is an underused feature on many web-based applications, but it will undoubtedly change the way you use Twitter by shortening the amount of time you spend looking for answers, resources, and people.

Figure 41-1

#42 Filter Your Twitter Search

When you search for a term, Twitter will give you a variety of options related to your search. For example, when you search for "#Satchat" (Figure 42-1), you'll see a menu bar above the search results (Figure 42-2).

Figure 42-1

Figure 42-2

From the menu bar, you can choose from several options:

Top lists the top Tweets (those that have been Retweeted and favorited) associated with the search term.

Live shows the live stream for your search term. This is what you want to use when you're participating in a chat that is using a specific hashtag. (See #50 Participate in a Subject-Specific Chat for more information on Twitter chats.)

Accounts shows the profiles most closely associated with your search term. This is a good tab to use if you want to expand your PLN. If you find a topic or hashtag you like, search for it, and then follow some of the people who show up under Accounts.

Photos shows the photos Tweeted using your search term.

Videos lists the videos that users have shared with the search term in the title or description. This is a great feature to use to find instructional or informational videos about your search.

More options provides you with additional search options (Figure 42-3).

Here are the types of items your search term will display for you.

All gives you everything associated with your search term.

Tweets only shows you Tweets posted with the search term.

Accounts gives you Twitter accounts that use the search term.

Photos shows you the photos with your search term.

Videos gives you the videos with the search term.

News gives you the news associated with the search term.

Whose Twitter pages do you want to search for the term in? You can pick everyone or just the people you follow.

Twitter also gives you the option of selecting the geographical area you want your search results from. Choose to see search results from everywhere, or only those near you.

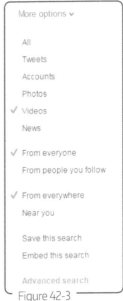

Figure 42-3

You can save your search and embed it into either a Tweet or a website.

Advanced search allows you to filter your search results even further.

#43 Take Advantage of Twitter Shortcuts

With so much to do, set up, and adjust to get your Twitter account up and running, you are probably curious about shortcuts, which just happen to be the most underutilized part of Twitter. Figure 43-1 shows you some of the shortcuts that can help you use Twitter more efficiently. You must be logged into Twitter on your device to get these shortcuts to work.

Figure 43-1

#44 Use Text Messaging in Lieu of the Twitter App

Maybe you do not have access to the Internet or a smartphone, but still want to stay in the loop with all that's going on in the Twitter world. Did you know that you can sign up to receive Twitter notifications as text messages?

Go to *Settings* and click the *Mobile* tab (Figure 44-1). On your smartphone, you'll find *Mobile Notifications* under the *Account* link. From there, select when you want to receive text messages that contain Tweets.

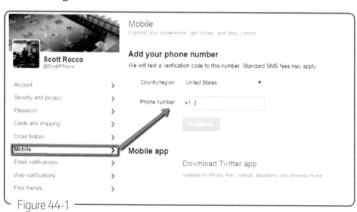

Figure 44-1

#45 Download the Twitter App on Your Smartphone

Why not become a mobile, connected educator and add the Twitter app to your smartphone? To download the Twitter app, go to the App Store if you have an iPhone. Visit Google Play if you use Android, or check out the Windows Store if you have a Windows phone. Simply search for "Twitter" and download the app.

Once the app is on your phone, sign in to your Twitter account. Once you've logged in, go to *Settings* and then click *Notifications tab* to select when and how you want to be notified about Tweets, DMs, interactions, and new followers. Be sure to turn off notifications if you do not want to constantly receive them.

#46 Never Tell an Educator They Must Use Twitter

We hope the first section has helped you become a connected educator and that you are finding value in using Twitter. In fact, we understand if you want to run out and tell every colleague that they *must* become connected and they *must* use Twitter. But as we conclude Section I, we want to give you this word of caution: Being a connected educator is more about modeling the right behaviors (sharing information, participating in chats, seeking out and growing your PLN) and less about telling people how they should grow professionally.

Once you catch Twitter fever, it's important to pick your spots for telling people how great it is. When you're sharing a wonderful idea or strategy, let your colleagues know you learned about it from another like-minded educator on Twitter. The more you give credit where credit is due and you model what it means to be a connected educator, the more your colleagues will start to understand Twitter's potential for educators. Remember, sharing is contagious and, ultimately, we grow as individuals when we learn from one another, and it affects the success of all students.

Another great approach to showing your colleagues the power of Twitter in education is to sit down with them and go through the sign-up process. Walk them through the steps of searching for information and resources they're interested in. Showing others how they can connect with respected educators around the world is a far more effective approach to take than simply telling them that they have to use Twitter.

Section I Conclusion ... One Tweet at a Time!

You've set up your Twitter account, determined your background, written your profile, and now you're Tweeting. We believe Twitter is an essential tool for every modern-day educator. If you're new to Twitter, it may take a little getting used to, but hang in there! The more familiar you become, the easier it will be to find the people and information that will help you grow as an educator.

Learning is a never-ending process; it's how we improve, and it's how we help our students succeed. We've given you the basics. Now we'll work on taking your social media skills to the next level by connecting, learning, and collaborating through Twitter, one Tweet at a time.

SECTION 2
TAKING TWITTER TO A HIGHER LEVEL

Now that you have the basics of Twitter down and are feeling comfortable posting Tweets and Retweets, it's time to learn more about what Twitter can do for you as an educator. We will take you through some of the platform's more complex features and explain how to connect Twitter with educational technology and other social media services you may already use. We will also help you go from simply consuming information to creating and sharing information.

Section II is all about taking Twitter to the next level, so let's get started!

#47 Tag Your PLN on Follow Friday (#FF)

Let's start this section with a fun tradition we partake in every Friday on Twitter: "Follow Friday." Educators who want to acknowledge a valuable person or group of people in their PLN will post #FF and then those individuals' names. Many people make it fun by adding a comment or picture associated with their #FF.

Some of our favorite #FF Tweets come from John Gunnell (@gunnellAP), principal of Jack Young Middle School in Baraboo, Wisconsin, who always compares his PLN to the title of a song (Figure 47-1, 47-2).

Participating in #FF is a nice way to say thank you to your PLN. It's also a great way to build your PLN; check the people other educators Tweet about on Follow Friday—and follow them. If you decide to post your own #FF Tweets, have fun and be creative!

John Gunnell @gunnellAP · Mar 4

This Magic Moment, my PLN rocks like Jay & the Americans @cybraryman1 @mikelubelfeld @drjolly @TonySinanis @gcouros @GustafsonBrad @johnkao

Figure 47-1

John Gunnell @gunnellAP · Mar 4

Hey Ho, Let's Go, my PLN rocks like The Ramones @ToddWhitaker @burgessdave @RickWormeli @kenoc7 @tguskey @BrianNC0506 @MaryMjelde @Braz74

Figure 47-2

#48 Join a Twitter Chat

At this point, you may be interested in participating in a Twitter chat. Chats aren't complex at all. Simply think of something you're interested in, like leadership in the school setting, and do a little research using the Twitter search box.

For example, if you type in keywords like "leadership" or "innovation," you more than likely will come across #Satchat, a Twitter chat for current and emerging school leaders that we host every Saturday morning. We have been consistent in holding the chat almost every single Saturday since 2012. On Saturdays that we don't hold a #Satchat, we have Jenny Grabiec (@techgirlgenny), Director of Technology at the Fletcher School, New York, and Ross Cooper (@RossCoops31), Supervisor of Instructional Practice in Salisbury Township, Pennsylvania, run #Satchathack.

To participate (or at least lurk) in a #Satchat, go to your Twitter search box and type "#Satchat." A feed will then come up with all of the Tweets using that hashtag. For an hour each Saturday, this hashtag is used solely for discussing an educational topic, and you will notice things like "Q1" (Question 1) and "A1" (Answer 1). This structure helps us organize the discussion so people can follow along and pop in at any time to share their insights.

If you're new to Twitter, you may feel hesitant about participating in the discussion. "What if nobody reads my Tweet?" Or better yet, "What if somebody disagrees with me?" Or worse, "What if one of my students or parents sees what I'm Tweeting?" Don't worry about it! As long as you keep your Tweets professional, positive, and beneficial, the rest will take care of itself. Just make sure to include #Satchat in your Tweet so that it becomes part of the discussion thread. Who knows? Your Tweet just may help another educator and their students.

Take a look at Figure 48-1 and the thread from one #Satchat conversation.

Figure 48-1

33

#49 Follow These Ten Twitter Chats

Through the use of topic-specific hashtags, Twitter provides educators the opportunity to get together and collaborate beyond the school day, faculty room, and professional development workshop.

Here are ten active and engaging Twitter chats to follow, along with their corresponding hashtags and meeting times. (All times listed are Eastern.) Please keep in mind that these chats will periodically take a week off depending on the schedule of their moderators. However, on any given day, you will find them running at the time listed below.

Sunday

5:30 a.m. - #aussieEd (Australia Education Chat)

9:00 a.m. - #Sunchat (Sunday Chat)

Monday

7:00 p.m. - #sschat (Social Studies Chat)

9:00 p.m. - #COLchat (Culture of Learning Chat)

9:00 p.m. - #tlap (Teach Like a PIRATE Chat)

Tuesday

8:30 p.m. - (*Every other Tuesday*) #NJED
(New Jersey Educators Chat)

Thursday

9:00 p.m. - #ArkEdChat (Arkansas Education Chat)

8:00 p.m. - #MSChat (Middle School Chat)

9:00 p.m. - (*Every other Thursday*) #EDTherapy
(Educational Therapy Chat)

Saturday

7:30 a.m. - #Satchat (Saturday Chat)

> If you are looking for a specific Twitter chat, visit https://sites.google.com/site/Twittereducationchats/

#50 Participate in a Subject-Specific Chat

As educators, we want to connect with those who teach the same grade or subject. What better way to connect with teachers in your subject area, outside of your school or district, than through Twitter? Join your extended subject-specific family on Twitter and grow as an educator as your PLN expands.

If you teach social studies, check out #sschat on Monday nights at 7 (ET) and connect with other social studies teachers. Do you know a fourth-grade teacher? Encourage them to search for #4thchat every Monday night at 8 (ET). Looking to meet your gifted learners' needs? Hop on over to #gtchat at 8 (ET) on Friday nights. There is a chat for everyone.

> If you are looking for a specific Twitter chat, visit https://sites.google.com/site/Twittereducationchats/

#51 New Teacher Resource: #ntchat

Years ago, new teachers were left to swim alone in the ocean, trying to keep their heads above water. Staying on top of best practices and dealing with the pressures of being a new teacher are incredibly hard tasks. Fast-forward to today, and social media has made it easier than ever for new teachers to connect with like-minded educators and gain access to innovative resources.

One example is the New Teachers Chat (#ntchat), which offers a wealth of resources for those new to our profession. Every Wednesday, from 8:00 to 9:00 p.m. (ET), new teachers chat about topics relevant to them. During the chat, you will also find experienced teachers and administrators joining in to add to the conversation.

#52 Looking to Grow Professionally? Check out #PersonalizedPD.

Twitter is a great place to grow professionally. If you are really into unique and innovative ways to improve your craft, then the #PersonalizedPD hashtag is the way to go. It's based off the book *Personalized PD: Flipping Your Professional Development*, published by the Bretzmann Group. Brad is one of the contributing authors as well. The chat takes place on Twitter every Tuesday at 9:00 p.m. (ET). Topics range from ways to leverage the power of technology to grow as an educator to discussing obstacles within the professional development process. Hop onto Twitter, type in the #PersonalizedPD hashtag, and explore all of the great ideas and resources shared on a daily basis.

#53 Follow a Conference Virtually

Hundreds of educational conferences and Edcamps—a participant-driven professional development opportunity organized, focused, and led by educators—are held each year around the world, but there is no way you can attend each and every one. Twitter can help you with that by providing opportunities to follow and learn from conference speakers from the comfort of your couch, classroom desk, or a seat on the soccer field sidelines.

For example, if you didn't make it to the 2016 NASSP Conference in Orlando, Florida, hop on over to Twitter, type "#nassp16" in the search box, and experience the conference through attendees' Tweets, images, video footage, memorable quotes, and shared information. In 2015, its inaugural year, Evolving Educators' Tomorrow's Classrooms Today Conference kept virtual participants in the loop using #TCT15. And you can do the same for other large conferences, including those hosted by the International Society for Technology in Education (ISTE), the Association for Supervision and Curriculum Development (ASCD), Learning Forward, and the National Association of Elementary School Principals (NAESP), to name just a few. The organization or conference website will generally post the event hashtag so you know what to search for. And if you follow educators or speakers who attend the events, you'll see the hashtags and you'll want to search for them in their Tweets.

#54 Tweet from an Educational Conference

If you have the opportunity to attend an educational conference, make Twitter your go-to resource. Taking notes via Twitter at an educational conference is truly an experience. For some Twitter users, Tweeting key ideas is a great way to not only keep track of what they're learning during the event, but also a chance to share those ideas with educators around the globe.

Typically, conferences will have a hashtag that participants can use to bring attention to all of the great things that they are experiencing. For example, at the annual Tomorrow's Classrooms Today Conference, participants use #TCT and then the year of the conference. In 2015, we used #TCT15, #TCT16 was the hashtag for

2016, and so on. Year after year, attendees use the hashtag of the conference to push out content to their followers through social media and transfer the learning experience at the conference to those who cannot attend.

Whether you are attending a small or large conference, take a few moments to share your insights on key takeaways from a session or keynote, post photos or short videos, or Tweet some powerful quotes from speakers. Educators cannot attend every conference, so they really appreciate the opportunity to follow along virtually. The next time you attend a conference, make sure to find out what the hashtag is and share what you learn via Twitter.

#55 Meet Your Virtual PLN in Person

Connecting with others and growing your PLN in the virtual world is fantastic. Meeting those people in person at a conference is even better! It is amazing that when you meet a member of your PLN in person, it feels like you're seeing an old friend because you have already connected and (hopefully) collaborated. That awkward moment of meeting someone is replaced by a handshake, hug, or high five.

Large conferences often live stream Tweets on a large screen, so try and attend a larger conference and introduce yourself to members of your PLN that you have never met in person. Sometimes those connections lead to amazing conversations, opportunities, and collaborative projects.

Being a connected educator really does have its perks.

#56 Promote an Educational Event with Twitter

Think of Twitter as a big bulletin board for educators, where you and your followers can read about and promote upcoming events. As you follow, attend, and present at conferences, make sure to share the conference information with your PLN on Twitter.

Promoting your educational event through Twitter is simple, but make sure you include a date, location, and website to visit for more information. You could even include the event's official hashtag if you know it (Figure 56-1). Google URL Shortener can help you stay under the 140-character limit by shortening the event's website address.

Pinned Tweet

Billy Krakower @wkrakower · 13 Nov 2015
Come to #TCT16 on May 21, 2016 at @RiderSchoolofEd Sign Up Today: buff.ly/1kROUOf #Satchat #highered #k12 #njed

Figure 56-1

#57 Create a Backchannel for Your Presentation

Today's professional development workshops need to create a buzz or interest outside the event that carries the learning and conversation beyond the moment. One way you can do this is by creating a "backchannel" for your presentation. This is a fancy way of asking participants and those out in the Twitterverse to discuss, ask questions, and collaborate using your hashtag.

If you are at a conference that's using a hashtag, by all means, feel free to use it to create your backchannel. But if the conference doesn't have one or if you want a backchannel exclusively for your presentation, then create your own hashtag.

For example, when Scott gave a keynote address to Rutgers University's Center for Effective School Practices, he listed his backchannel's hashtag on his opening slide

Using Social Media to Support Professional Learning and Effective Instruction
Scott Rocco, Ed.D.
@ScottRRocco
Saturday, March 7, 2015
Backchannel:
#RUGSEAR

RUTGERS
Alternate Route

Figure 57-1

(Figure 57-1), and in his introduction, he asked conference participants to use the hashtag to discuss the presentation and provide feedback. Those Tweets helped ensure the discussion and learning continued long after his keynote ended.

#58 Build Up Your Twitter Stamina

One of the most common misconceptions people have when they start a Twitter account is that they need to Tweet a lot. Well, you do need to Tweet consistently to increase your PLN and develop a presence, but you also need to find your Tweeting groove.

We hope you're already Tweeting at least once a day. Over time, you will probably want to post a few times daily. Along the way, you will discover a level of sending and reading Tweets with which you're comfortable—this is your Twitter stamina. Maybe you have five or ten minutes to devote to connecting via Twitter daily. Finding the right balance of posting Tweets, consuming information via Tweets, and collaborating with your PLN will take some time, but as time goes on, your Twitter stamina will increase. For now, though, the following page features our suggestions for developing your Twitter stamina.

#59 Retweet Daily

Part of being a connected educator is sharing what you read and learn from others. Retweeting at least once a day is a simple way to do that. Retweeting daily provides your followers with quality information and lets your PLN know you think what they are providing is valuable. Remember, however, the first rule of Retweeting is to *always* review the original Tweet—read the linked article, view the whole image, watch the entire video—before you Retweet it.

Also remember that when you Retweet, you have about 116 characters to make a comment about whatever it is that you are Retweeting. Users on mobile devices have the ability to "quote Tweet" or "Retweet" through the Twitter app.

Figure 59-1 shows an example in which Scott Retweeted and commented on a Tweet. You can see Scott Retweeted above the original Tweet and added "RT." Although Twitter is making it easier to Retweet, you should still add the "RT."

On the next page, you will see an example of a Tweet from Starr Sackstein (@mssackstein) that Brad wants to Retweet and comment on (Figure 59-2). Typically, Twitter will give users about 116 characters when adding a Retweet with a comment. In the example of a Tweet by Brad that Scott Retweeted, Scott decided not to add a comment and just Retweeted (Figure 59-3). We have found that Retweets get more action if a comment is added.

Figure 59-1

Figure 59-2

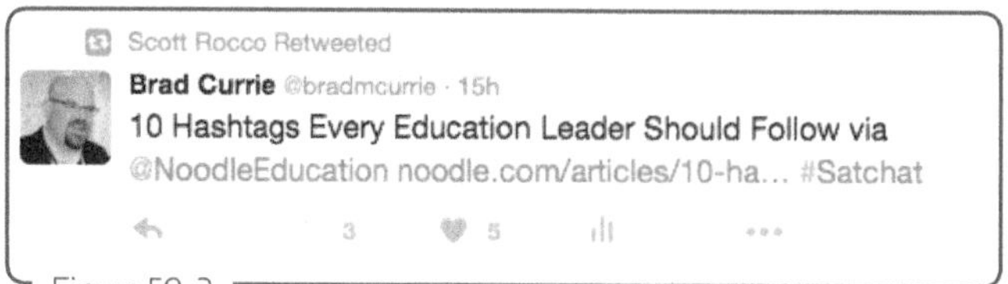

Figure 59-3

#60 Post and Quote Tweets Daily

It's also a good idea to quote Tweet daily. What is the difference between a quote Tweet and a Retweet? When you click the double arrow to Retweet a post, Twitter gives you the option of adding a comment—this becomes your quote Tweet.

In Figure 60-1, you could add a comment like, "Check out #EdCampNJ and register today!" Click *Retweet*, and your quote Tweet is ready to roll.

Figure 60-1

#61 Twitter Regimen

One of Brad's more popular blog posts discusses being a connected educator and how we can build our Twitter stamina. The following is an excerpt from that post that should help you build your PLN and increase your knowledge as a connected educator. You can read Brad's blog in its entirety by visiting his website: http://www.bradcurrie.net/blog/connect-yourself-before-you-wreck-yourself.

Connect Yourself Before You Wreck Yourself

Month One

- Log on to Twitter and consume information twice a week for about twenty minutes at a clip.
- Follow ten new educators every week.

Month Two

- Continue Month One's regimen and ...
- Tweet links, articles, ideas, videos, and resources.

Month Three

- Continue the regimens from Months One and Two, plus ...
- Join a Twitter chat such as #Satchat, #ntchat, #tlap, #COLchat, and #sschat

Month Four

- Continue the regimens from Months One, Two, and Three, plus ...
- Promote the importance of expanding your PLN with your peers.
- Model all that is great with Twitter and other web-based professional development (PD).

Month Five

- Continue the regimens from Months One, Two, Three, and Four, plus ...
- Integrate Twitter into your classroom or school as a way to engage your students, promote student and staff achievements, and inform school stakeholders.

#62 Pin a Tweet to Your Profile Page

As you build your Twitter stamina, you will post more and more Tweets that express your views on education, our profession, and teaching-specific topics. Now, thanks to the addition of a recent Twitter feature, you can pin a Tweet that helps identify who you are as an educator to your profile page, further enhancing the great profile you put together in Section I.

To pin a Tweet, pick one that you have posted that centers on your beliefs or something you're working toward. At the bottom of that Tweet, click the icon with three dots (Figure 62-1).

Figure 62-1

Select the *Pin to your profile page* option. Once you do, the Tweet will be at the top of your Tweet history and be labeled "Pinned Tweet" (Figure 62-2). You can only pin one Tweet at a time. If you so choose, you can unpin by clicking the three little dots and selecting *Unpin*.

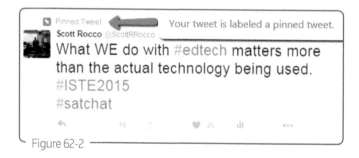

Figure 62-2

#63 Create a Classroom Twitter Handle

The ability for a teacher to change the dinner conversation at home with a simple Tweet is very powerful. As a parent, Brad truly appreciates the effort that his son's fourth-grade teacher, Laurie Ann Moore (@MrsMooreFRSD), puts into managing her classroom's Twitter handle. Almost nightly, right before dinner, Brad can log on to Twitter and see what his son experienced in class (Figure 63-1). Instead of asking him, "How was school today?" he instead can say, "I see you worked on personal narratives in class. What were some things you wrote about?" To Brad, this is a game-changer in education. If a teacher does not tell their classroom story, somebody else might. And it could be wrong.

Figure 63-1

To set up your classroom's very own Twitter handle:

1. Ask your building administrator for permission. (Or beg for forgiveness later and just do it!)
2. Register your Twitter handle. Choose one that incorporates your name, grade level, and/or subject matter.
3. Tweet at least once a day or a couple times a week for consistency.
4. Let your parents know that you will use Twitter to tell your classroom's story. Encourage them to check in regularly to see what their kids are up to.

Tip: Post pictures of students (following your school's privacy guidelines, of course) and of the fun things that are going on in your classroom.

#64 Start a Classroom Hashtag

Hashtags are a big part of how people find information and bring attention to what matters in the social media world. During the past few years, classrooms, schools, and districts have leveraged the power of hashtags as they tell their stories via social media. Engaging stakeholders, particularly parents, in the virtual world is smart! It's an effective way to communicate, given the fact that most carry smartphones with them at all times and want real-time information. Enter Twitter.

Just like maintaining a classroom Twitter handle can help keep parents and students in the loop, so can a classroom hashtag. Imagine how powerful a classroom hashtag would be across all social media platforms, including Instagram, Facebook, and Twitter! At any point in time, on any platform, a parent or student could search for the hashtag and see stories, photos, updates, even video. Tools like Tagboard.com can help you accomplish the task of following a hashtag across multiple social media sites at one time. After signing up for Tagboard, parents can simply type in your classroom's hashtag and find out what's happening in real time.

When creating a classroom hashtag, consider something easy to remember and related to your name, school, or mascot. Then make sure your students and parents know what the hashtag is—tweet about it!

#65 Tweet from a Field Trip

Tweeting from a field trip is a great way to share places that other educators may not have the opportunity to experience for themselves. You could coordinate a virtual field trip for another classroom and have your students share photos and what you are learning. Other teachers and students can then respond to your Tweets and ask questions. By the way, this works both ways! You can have your class take a virtual field trip with students from another class as their guides.

#66 Assign Homework through Twitter

As teachers, we are always trying to find cool ways to assign homework. With a classroom Twitter handle or hashtag, you can provide your students with real-time homework updates—and make homework cool.

Just have your students log on to Twitter (or use their smartphone Twitter app), locate your classroom handle or hashtag, scroll to find the assignment, and then complete the work. You can incorporate links, videos, documents, images, and polls into a homework Tweet to provide the topic at hand with additional educational value.

#67 Assess Your Students' Knowledge Using Hashtags

Not only can you use Twitter to help you further your own professional growth as an educator, but you can also use it to assess your students' comprehension of a topic.

Say, for instance, you are a high school teacher preparing a social studies lesson on the American Revolution and you want to gather student insight. Rather than holding an old-fashioned, whole class discussion, have your students take out their devices and Tweet their thoughts using the classroom hashtag. As an extra touch, project the Twitter discussion onto your SMART Board for all to see.

Sometimes we, as educators, can be reluctant to encourage students to participate in an "uncontrolled" conversation because we're afraid that a student might Tweet something inappropriate. This is totally understandable, but don't underestimate your students' ability to rise up and leverage the power of social media in a positive way. Modeling the appropriate use of Twitter and setting clear ground rules will hopefully alleviate any issues that may arise.

If an issue does come up, treat it as if you would any other code of conduct violation or classroom behavior issue: Have a private discussion with the student and reach out to his or her parents, if warranted. In extreme cases, you may notify your administration as well.

When teachers take risks, students will take risks. Using Twitter to assess your students' understanding is definitely a risk worth taking. And you might even discover that the shy student who never speaks up in class has quite a lot to say when given the chance to virtually voice her thoughts.

#68 Tweet Sports Scores

HV Girls Basketball @HVGBBall · Mar 4
Article: Hopewell girls cruise past Long Branch to reach CJ III quarters
trentonian.com//sports/201503…

Figure 68-1

The Tweet in Figure 68-1 says it all. Twitter has become such a prevalent part of our culture that professional and school athletic departments, teams, and athletes now keep their fans up-to-date on the latest news in 140 characters or less. Twitter has even changed the way newspaper reporters reach their audiences and how teams tell their stories. For example, instead of waiting for the game to be over and reading about in the next day's local newspaper, people can follow a writer on Twitter who might be at the game live-tweeting updates.

Before you start a Twitter handle for your school's athletics department, get approval from your administration. Provide examples from your Twitter feed to show decision makers the power that Twitter has to inform virtual stakeholders. It's also a great way to connect with former players and alumni.

And if you really want to get creative, consider live streaming events using the Periscope app so that family members and friends unable to attend games can watch them on their devices.

#69 Listen to Student Voice

Student voice—their insights, opinions, and experiences—is one of the most critical components in a school's success. Educators on Twitter are bringing attention to it by using the #stuvoice hashtag. All day, every day, educators from around the globe are sharing insights and resources pertaining to student voice.

Listening to our students is important because their input can help us improve learning experiences and school culture. If you do a Twitter search using the #stuvoice hashtag, you will come across so many wonderful resources, like Bob Dillion's (@ideaguy42) Tweet about student voice during an #iaedchat (Iowa Education Chat) Twitter discussion (Figure 69-1). Listen and choose to learn from #stuvoice.

Bob Dillon @ideaguy42 · 19h
A1: My hope comes from the #stuvoice that is demanding a new way to learn. #iaedchat

Figure 69-1

#70 Tell Your School's Story

As much as Twitter can connect classrooms, it can also help elementary, middle, and high schools as well as school districts connect with parents and the community.

Using its Twitter handle, a school can push out news about everything from sports scores to classroom learning experiences and after-school club events—almost anything, really—as long as the focus is on students. For example, one Tweet could say, "Students in Mrs. Currie's language arts class use Google Docs' voice-to-text feature to help improve their writing skills." You could then include a photo showing the students involved in this learning experience. It really is that simple, and you know what? School stakeholders appreciate the insight.

Think about it. What other time in the history of education have schools been able to provide this sort of window into the school's daily happenings? No doubt social media has helped make this one of the most exciting times in education.

Scott wrote about just this after he gave a keynote at the Alaska Principals' Conference in Anchorage. The following is his blog post on this topic: http://www.edsocialmedia. com/2014/11/whos-telling-story/.

Who's Telling Our Story

On October 21, 2014, I had the honor and privilege of giving the keynote address at the Alaska Principals' Conference in Anchorage. The theme of the conference was "Telling Our Story," and my focus was "Who's Telling Our Story: The Use of Social Media in Education." The conference theme was a brilliant concept, because as our educational system changes, it becomes increasingly vital that educators, specifically principals and district administrators, tell our educational stories. Here is a brief glimpse into some of the main points from my keynote.

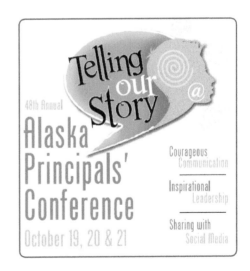

Who is telling our story? This question is based on media coverage of education. It is extremely rare to see a front page, above-the-fold story about education that is positive. Our current status, with respect to news stories published about education, is negative, and the five major online news organizations (Fox, CNN, CBS, NBC, and ABC) do not have a link on their main page to educational information. This is neither

negative nor conspiracy theorizing—it's simply a fact related to the world we live in and the issues we face globally. Take a look and see for yourself. Therefore, if the press doesn't put education on the front page of the newspaper or provide a tab on their main page, why tell our story?

This was the question I posed to my PLN on Twitter prior to the keynote, and here are three summarized responses:

1. ***If we don't, someone else will.*** Well, that has some validity, but I think it could be rephrased to say, "If we don't, no one else will." So this is a reason, but not the real reason.

2. ***It's the only good press we will get.*** At times it may feel like this, and my history of reading stories in the paper would find this to be rather accurate. But this is not the real reason, either.

3. ***Great things happen in our schools every day.*** Think about that. Think about your classroom(s), school, students, staff, and community. Each and every day, something great goes on in our schools. This is the real reason why we tell our educational story.

Every day in our schools, there are stories of hard work paying off. Students overcoming challenges. Teachers working to make a connection with students who haven't found their place in school. Schools providing community service in our towns and cities. Academics and athletics succeeding as individuals, groups, and teams. Schools and communities working together. It's there—every day—in each of our schools, and the stories deserve to be told. Not for the glory. Not to be smug. But to recognize effort, success, hard work, and the fact that great things are happening in our schools and most people have no idea.

But how do we tell our educational story and talk about the great things that transpire? We do it through storytelling, but we take the modern-day version of storytelling and make it digital through social media. We do this because using social media to tell our educational stories of the great things happening in our schools every day provides an opportunity for our schools to do the following:

- *Interact with our community*
- *Create and share information about what's happening in our schools*
- *Engage our stakeholders and allow us to socially interact with them*

One of the challenges in using social media tools for digital storytelling is deciding where to begin. As complex as this may sound, with all the different options, it's a rather simple answer: Just pick one. Don't get hung up on a social media app, site, or program. Just pick one, post relevant content for your community members, and you will begin to connect, share, and collaborate with them.

So who is telling our story? We are! We are sharing the great things occurring every day in our schools by using social media for digital storytelling. Your students, staff, and community deserve to hear these educational stories. Give it a try and let us know how it goes.

#71 Engage Parents

Let's get right to the point: parents expect their children's school to communicate with them virtually. There's no hiding from it. Luckily, Twitter can do wonders for informing parents of school happenings, disseminating important information, and promoting student and staff achievements. Doing a simple thing like Tweeting from a classroom or school Twitter handle will go a long way in promoting the success of students and building a positive school culture. Students and staff love to be recognized, and you can never inform people too much. Remember, if you do not tell your school or classroom story, someone else will, and it could be wrong.

Once the Twitter handle for your classroom, school, or district is up and running, promote it through email blasts and website updates.

Figure 71-1

Also, make sure to have your school's Twitter feed visible on your website. As your follower base grows, so will the buzz within your community of parents. The joy parents receive from getting a glimpse at what their child is experiencing in school is, in a word, priceless. Tweets like the one in Figure 71-1 go a long way toward building strong parent-teacher relationships.

As your school's Twitter account takes off, staff members, students, and parents will hop on the Twitter train and ask for moments to be Tweeted. Consistency is key when trying to reach an audience with Twitter, and we recommend Tweeting at least twice a day to draw attention to the great things going on in your school or district.

Follow the Rules

Always remember to follow your school's privacy guidelines regarding photos. Some districts may require that parents and students sign social media release forms.

#72 Engage Community Members on Twitter

As important as it is for us to engage parents through Twitter, it's equally as important that we engage community members. Any time members of the community visit your school or your students are out in the community, whether it's Career Day, Mystery Location calls, Cultural Diversity Day, Veterans Day, police safety presentations, guest readers, or local grant awards, Tweet about it. The publicity is good for both your school and the community, and it could lead to bigger and better things down the road.

If it benefits students, it's worth Tweeting about!

#73 Start a District Twitter Handle

Picture this: A small school district in Anytown, USA, that has yet to consider the possibilities of using social media to communicate with its community. It decides it needs to quickly get with the times and meet stakeholders in the virtual world. So the district takes a risk and leverages the power of social media. It transforms its website, makes digital newsletters the norm for staff, and creates a brand-spanking-new Twitter handle. To generate a buzz among students, staff, and parents, in addition to traditional methods, the superintendent announces a snow day via Twitter. The rest is history.

From district-wide sports scores to school power outage updates, Twitter gives us the opportunity to provide timely information to our districts' constituents with a couple of clicks of the mouse or taps on a mobile device.

Spotswood Schools
@SPSChargers

⚡ The official Twitter account for Spotswood Public Schools. Promoting the excellent things happening every day in our schools. ⚡

📍 Spotswood, NJ 🔗 spsd.us

Figure 73-1

Take a look at what New Jersey's Spotswood Public Schools (@SPSChargers) has done with its Twitter feed (Figures 73-1 and 2). In the past few years alone, the district has gained almost a thousand followers—and more are following all the time.

Consistency, relevancy, and student-centered Tweets create a surefire recipe for any district to successfully communicate and build connections both within the school and with the community at large.

Spotswood Schools @SPSChargers · Nov 7
Congrats Football team on your second consecutive Blue Division Championship!

↩   ↻ 16   ♥ 25   •••

Figure 73-2

#74 School Twitter Handles

School Twitter handles are critical in order to engage stakeholders in the virtual world. "Why?" you might ask. You can inform followers of school happenings, promote student and staff achievements, and push traffic back to your school's website. It's just one more way to differentiate your school's message and ensure no stakeholder is left behind. Here are a few schools we follow:

School Name	Twitter Handle
Black River Middle School	@BlackRiverMS
Timberview Middle School	@TimberViewMS
Bettendorf High School	@U_Bett
William Davies Middle School	@WilliamDaviesMS
Central Cabot Elementary School	@CentralCabotpK4

#75 Manage Multiple Twitter Accounts with Your Smartphone

You have your personal Twitter account, and, at this point, you may want to develop an account for your class, school, district, organization, or business. That means managing multiple accounts. Trust us, this sounds more complex than it really is. We each have at least two, if not three, accounts that we manage at any given time.

To add a new or existing account, tap *More options* at the bottom of your screen, select the appropriate choice, and let Twitter walk you through the process (Figure 75-1).

In Figure 75-1, you can see Scott's Twitter account on his iPhone. Tap the people icon, and you will see a list of all the accounts you manage, with the white checkmark inside the green circle identifying which account is active on your app. You can see from Billy's screenshot of his Android phone that the process of choosing which account to Tweet from is similar (Figure 75-2).

Tap the account name you want, and the checkmark moves to that account.

Note: Be very careful. Managing multiple accounts means you have a better chance of Tweeting the wrong thing to the wrong Twitter followers, so be sure to identify which account you want to use. To delete an account from your list, tap *Edit* (Figure 75-3).

Tap it. Go ahead—it will be fine! When you do, you will see the menu in Figure 75-4.

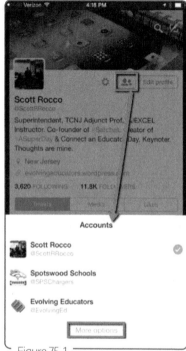

Figure 75-1

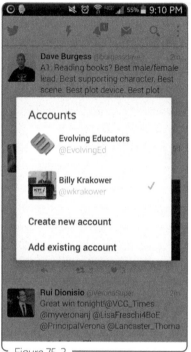

Figure 75-2

Tap the red circle with the minus sign in it that appears next to the account you want to remove, and Twitter will ask if you want to remove it. If you do, tap *Remove*. If you don't, tap *Done*. If you accidently delete an account, you can easily add it back.

Figure 75-3

Figure 75-4

#76 Host Twitter Tutorials for Your Colleagues

Bringing your colleagues onto the Twitter boat can be a daunting task, so consider conducting Twitter tutorials in person or virtually using Google Hangouts.

If you decide to do sessions in person, make yourself available for brief pockets of time before, during, or after school in a space with a projector so that participants can clearly see what you are talking about. It's perfectly fine if only one person shows up to a session—the point is to help your fellow educators understand the power that lies in connecting with each other and sharing best practices. You may also display a Twitter stream in your school's faculty room or in a large meeting area to show your colleagues who haven't signed up for a tutorial what Twitter can do. Google Hangouts is another viable method to get the word out about the benefits of Twitter. This real-time video meeting service is free and allows people to speak, listen to, and see each other on their computers or mobile devices. One of Google Hangouts' great features is the ability to share your screen with other people on the hangout. This comes in handy when trying to show a colleague how to use Twitter.

No matter how effective or ineffective an educator may be, everyone has at least one thing to share. And bottom line, the act of sharing is contagious, and ultimately, the shared *learning* affects students' success. The options are limitless when it comes to Twitter and what can be shared when trying to move people forward in the virtual world. Remember that videos, images, links, polls, and ideas can be Tweeted out.

#77 Manage Negative Comments

When a stakeholder Tweets negative comments about your class, school, or district, something everyone eventually encounters, you can do one of several things.

Your first option is to respond; however, be careful in your response, because you could incite a debate, and, no matter what, you won't win. If you can provide evidence to refute the Tweet and change someone's opinion, then consider providing it. However, the best response is to invite the individual to speak with you in person.

The second option is to do nothing. Many school social media feeds, including Twitter and Facebook, are designed to only put out information, not to respond to comments. This makes the decision clear in how you will or will not respond.

And third, if the post is completely inappropriate, we suggest calling the person and talking to them about their post. Using social media does not give any of us free rein to post anything we want without being held accountable for it. So if someone posts something very negative, they should not assume anonymity or that someone won't contact them about it.

#78 Promote Positive Twitter Use among Students

Using Twitter in your classroom and school is a great way to engage your colleagues, students, parents, and community members. It is also an opportunity to be a role model.

Leading by example in the virtual world is crucial if we want to be a positive influence on our students. So, let's be honest for a moment: The only reason people gripe about social media tools like Twitter is because they are sometimes used inappropriately. The more educators, and all adults for that matter, use Twitter as a means to have authentic conversations, share resources, and initiate positive change, the better off education will be in the long run.

What you Tweet as an educator matters, whether you think so or not, and stakeholders are paying attention to how you tell your story and consistently share best practices in the virtual world. These behaviors will eventually work their way down to your students, who can then try to have the same impact.

Take #stuvoice, the student voice hashtag we mentioned earlier, as an example. It has transformed the way people of all ages focus on the importance of having a student voice in education. The conversations arising from #stuvoice have helped make it very clear that when educational decisions take student voice into account, the school's culture improves and students get the learning environment they deserve.

With appropriate adult supervision, Twitter can make a profound impact on how students tell their stories and prepare for the real world.

#79 Include Your Blog or Website in Your Twitter Profile

Do you have a blog that would benefit other educators or that you want your parents and students to visit regularly? Bring attention to it by putting its link in your Twitter profile. Click the *Edit Profile* button (Figure 79-1) and add your link to your profile information (Figure 79-2).

Figure 79-1

Figure 79-2

#80 Share Your Blog on Twitter

Blogging is an awesome way to share an idea or concept with your PLN, and Twitter makes it easy to do this by allowing you to send out a blog post's link. The easiest way to share a link is to click the Twitter button at the bottom of your blog post. (Your blog uses a social media plugin, right? If not, add them now!)

When you or your readers are signed in to Twitter, a simple click will open a message window with the blog's title and link auto-populated (Figure 80-1).

Add a message and a few hashtags to spark your followers' interest in the post (Figure 80-2).

Then just click *Tweet* and you'll have shared your blog post!

Figure 80-1

Figure 80-2

#81 Add a Follow Button to Your Website or Blog

Engaging your Twitter audience on multiple platforms is an effective way to give you exposure on a number of fronts. Most website and blog services have a social media button option that you can activate with a few clicks or taps of the screen. Make sure your Twitter Follow button is prominently displayed on your website or blog.

In Figure 81-1, you can see how Brad Currie's website, BradCurrie.net, has multiple social media buttons for his visitors to access.

Figure 81-1

#82 Add a Share Button to Your Blog

You will want your blog posts to have a Twitter Share button, which allows readers to share your post with their followers on Twitter. Readers simply click the Twitter icon at the bottom of your post, log in to their Twitter account, modify the message, and post their Tweet. In Figure 82-1, Billy Krakower's blog post has a Twitter button located at end of it.

Figure 82-1

#83 Embed Tweets on Blogs and Websites

Don't assume your stakeholders or blog readers pay attention to every Tweet you and your organization push out. Embedding your Twitter feed on your website or blog goes a long way in getting your message out on multiple platforms.

Take, for example, Spotswood Public Schools' website, which has its Twitter feed prominently featured for site visitors to see (Figure 83-1).Twitter makes it very easy to add a widget to your blog:

Step 1: Log into Twitter and click on *Settings*.

Step 2: Click *Widgets* on lower left-hand side of the page.

Step 3: Click *Create new*.

Step 4: Configure your widget's look and feel.

Step 5: Copy and paste your widget's HTML into your website or blog's coding.

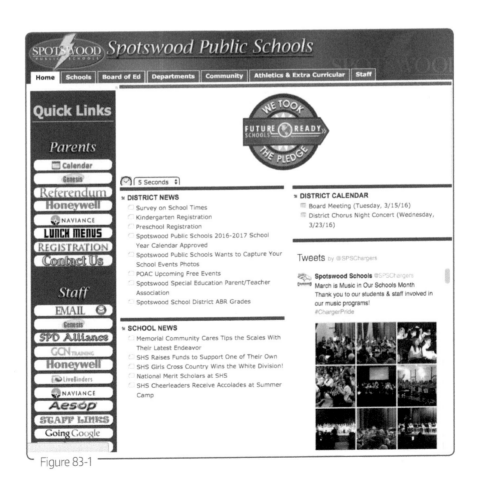

Figure 83-1

#84 Start a Hashtag for Your Book or Blog

Hashtags are a powerful way to promote a book, blog, or educational movement on Twitter. *New York Times* best-selling author Dave Burgess (@BurgessDave) did it for *Teach Like a PIRATE* using #tlap, and award-winning thought leader Eric Sheninger (@E_Sheninger) did it with his book, *Digital Leadership: Changing Paradigms for Changing Times*, using #digilead. Over time, these hashtags become more than a tool to promote a book or build a brand—they foster conversations and encourage sharing resources, ultimately supporting student success.

Case in point, the hashtag we will use for this book, #140EduTips. That's right! You heard it here first. We will use #140EduTips not only as a promotional tool for this book, but also to move the educational conversation forward in 140 characters or less.

Staying isolated is no longer an option for educators. Come out of your shell, connect on Twitter, and share all of the amazing work you do for students each and every day. Leverage the power of the #140EduTips hashtag to start conversations, share your best practice resources, and tell your story.

Getting into the Details of Your Twitter Use

#85 Track Your Followers and Unfollowers

Third-party applications like Crowdfire (CrowdfireApp.com) can assist you with keeping track of your followers, unfollowers, inactives (accounts of people who have not Tweeted in months), and other Twitter analytics. You can access the free version of the web-based application on any device with an Internet connection.

#86 Make a Twitter List

After you've been on Twitter for a while, you will start developing a strong arsenal of people who follow you (your followers) and those whom you actually follow (following).

People often ask us if they have to keep up with every Tweet from the people they follow, and the answer is no way—it would become overwhelming! That's where lists come in. Twitter allows you to create a list of people (separate from your main feed) whose Tweets you really want to follow and learn from. You can also curate lists of people you have met (or want to connect with) at educational conferences, lists of educators in your school or district, or lists of Twitter chat participants or bloggers you want to follow.

To create a list:

Step 1: Log on to your Twitter account.

Step 2: Click on your profile pic in the upper right-hand corner of the page.

Step 3: Click *Lists (Figure 86-1)*.

Step 4: Click *Create new list* on the right-hand side of page (Figure 86-2).

Step 5: Title your list. For example, "Evolving Educators."

Step 6: Write a brief description of what subscribers can expect, especially if you intend to make your list public.

Step 7: Determine if you want your list to be private or public.

Step 8: Save your list.

Step 9: Find an educator on Twitter and go to their profile page (Figure 86-3).

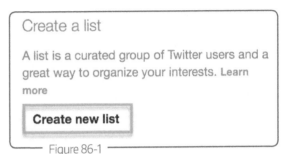

Figure 86-1

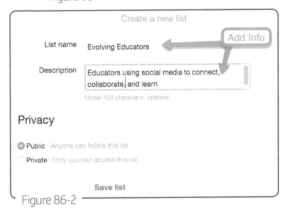

Figure 86-2

Figure 86-3

Step 10: Click the sprocket icon on the right-hand side of their page.

Step 11: Click Add/remove from lists (Figure 86-4).

Step 12: Select the list you want to add the person to.

Step 13: Repeat this process with others whom you want to add to your list(s).

Lists can be very powerful and help us use Twitter efficiently. Once you create a list, feel free to share it with others by copying and pasting the url of the list.

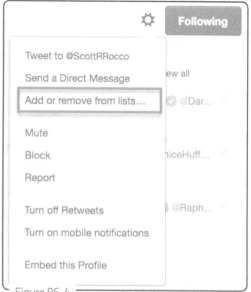

Figure 86-4

#87 Subscribe to a Twitter Education List

Educators on Twitter love to create lists so they can more easily focus on the people who inspire them to grow professionally. The list feature allows users to create a group of Twitter handles specific to their interests and needs. For example, if a user is interested in educational leadership, they can create and build a list of educational leaders on Twitter. Lists make it a whole lot easier to focus on specific topics and people.

Subscribing to lists is easy. To subscribe to a list, go to a user's profile page and find the *Lists* tab. Scan through the user's lists and click the list's link. On the next screen, you'll see Tweets from that list's members and a bit of info about the list. Click *Subscribe*.

Now, Tweets from people on the list will show up in your list feed, even if you don't follow them. You can always unsubscribe if you find a list isn't for you.

Contribute to the Greater Good on Twitter

#88 Share Other Educators' Work

We are huge proponents of sharing others' work more than our own. Each one of us is well-versed in a niche area—that's where our unique, original Tweets come from. The rest of our Tweets come from members of our PLN. These educators from around the world have expertise in specific subjects and areas that we can learn from, so theirs are the Tweets we share, the ones we find value in, and we think the rest of our PLN can find value in. Sharing these Tweets helps expand our followers' knowledge, all the while promoting other connected educators' efforts. And in the process, we increase our own knowledge in areas outside our niche.

As you share others' work, give them credit by including their handles in the Tweet or marking the Tweet as a Retweet or modified Tweet. You'll find educators appreciate when you share their work, but do not expect to receive a thank you. Sometimes educators will send you an appreciative Tweet for sharing their work, but they aren't expected to.

#89 Reply When Others Reach Out

One of the many unwritten rules in the Twitter world is that you do your best to reply or Tweet back to people who Tweet at you. A simple acknowledgment goes a long way.

Will there be times when you miss a Tweet or two? Absolutely. But the point is that you should try your best to connect in a timely fashion. Wouldn't it be great if there were a vacation responder for Twitter, similar to email? In any event, replying is good practice when you're trying to build your followership and bolster your virtual reputation.

You could also reach out to the person who contacted you via a direct message, a more private method that allows you to expand upon your public conversation.

You may encounter times when people challenge your way of thinking on Twitter, and that's perfectly fine. Just keep your cool and remain positive. If things get too crazy, ignore or block the person.

#90 Connect with Educators Around the World

Twitter has made the educational world flat. It has eliminated titles and put everyone on the same playing field, regardless of whether you're a teacher or an administrator. Want to reach out to a school leader from Australia? No problem. How about a teacher in Qatar? Like-minded educators are connecting on Twitter daily.

Every Saturday at 7:30 a.m. (ET), educators from around the world share their insights on a given topic using the hashtag #Satchat. For the three of us, as moderators of #Satchat, it has been so interesting seeing the passion people have for our profession. Way back in April 2012, Scott and Brad started #Satchat. Soon after Billy Krakower joined the team, and it has been going strong ever since. #Satchat has since expanded its family. On the West Coast, Shelley Burgess (@burgess_shelley) and Darin Jolly (@drjolly) moderate #SatchatWC at 7:30 a.m. (PST). #SatchatOZ (Australia) is moderated by Andrea Stringer and Tina Photakis, and is a prime example of educators sharing best practices and offering a global perspective on what matters most when trying to help students grow. #SatchatME (Middle East), moderated by Holly Fairbrother, Paul Fairbrother, Andrew McDonald, and Dan Pardy, offers educators another opportunity to participate in educational discussions with Twitter users from another part of the world.

Ultimately, where these chats originate doesn't matter; it's the conversations spanning continents that make you a better educator in the long run.

#91 Collaborate with Someone on Twitter

Pictured left to right:
Billy Krakower, Brad Currie, and Scott Rocco.
Photo courtesy of Kevin Jarrett.

Picture this: Three New Jersey educators from different walks of life decide in 2012 to start using Twitter. Little did they know that this decision would change their lives.

We were those three educators, and we were new to the Twitter landscape and wanted to start an online discussion for current and emerging school leaders. Finding a day and time that would allow people from around the world to participate in real time was tricky, but after much deliberation, we decided to have the Twitter chat every Saturday at 7:30 a.m. (ET). We named this one-of-a-kind Twitter discussion forum "#Satchat," and the rest is history.

We're proof that Twitter makes collaborating with other educators very easy. In fact, Billy often uses Twitter to find creative ideas he can use in his classroom. A great example of this kind of collaboration is Mystery Skype sessions or Mystery Location calls. When you want to find someone to do a project with, simply send out a Tweet using #MysterySkype or #MysteryLocationCalls, and you will get a response from someone who is willing to help (Figure 91-1).

Back in January 2012, Billy had really only just begun using Twitter when he decided it was time to try a Mystery

Figure 91-1

Call with his students. He sent out a Tweet similar to the one above, and Nancy Carroll (@NancyCarroll), an educator in Massachusetts, responded. Billy had connected with Nancy through his interactions on #4thchat (she is one of the co-moderators). The day for which they scheduled a Mystery Call happened to be the day after both the Giants and Patriots learned they would face each other in Super Bowl XLVI. Knowing that their respective schools were very close to the two teams' homes, Billy and Nancy decided to do another call right before the Super Bowl—and, of course, make a friendly wager. Billy and Nancy decided that it would be perfect if the students learned about Indianapolis, since that was the host Super Bowl site, and they would spilt the information between the two classes to have them do a report on the Friday before the Super Bowl. This became another way in which they were able to connect and move beyond the Mystery Call.

What began as an opportunity for their classes to do a Mystery Call turned into a collaborative relationship that includes other educators, all thanks to Twitter. They have worked together on a variety of projects, including Read Across America, learning about Mardi Gras, participating in and conducting surveys, working on weather assignments, and much more. Billy wrote about these and other projects in his book *Connecting Your Students to the World: Tools and Projects to Make Global Collaboration Come Alive, K-8.*

Opportunities abound for educators to collaborate on all sorts of initiatives and projects through Twitter. Consider reaching out to one of your followers or someone you follow and pitching an idea. You never know what might come of it.

#92 Seek Educational Advice on Twitter

Let's be honest for a moment: Whether you are a social studies teacher, department chairperson, or superintendent, no one knows everything there is to know about education. So how can we fill in the gaps when we need advice? Beyond asking a colleague down the hall or leaning on a mentor, turn to Twitter.

To ask a question, simply click *Compose* and begin typing your question, making sure to include a relevant hashtag, such as #sschat for a social studies question. Using hashtags increases the likelihood that you will receive an answer. You may also include someone's Twitter handle in your Tweet, especially if that person has a lot of followers, because the user could then Retweet your question and help you get an answer.

We often have educators from around the world reach out to us for advice, and all three of us consistently ask our PLN for their insights or pose questions to gather a consensus. We all understand that no matter how involved you are on Twitter or how many followers you have, everyone needs educational advice at some point. This is one of the many amazing things social media,

Scott Rocco @ScottRRocco · Sep 5
How do you...
insert a video into Google Classroom without using YouTube?

Figure 92-1

and specifically Twitter, offers educators.

A simple Tweet like the one from Scott in Figure 92-1 is a great way to ask for assistance and get help learning something new.

#93 Host a Booktalk via Twitter

Twitter has brought the education community together in ways once unimaginable. Years ago, you could only have a booktalk in person, but fast-forward to today, and educators can now discuss important topics mentioned in educational books online.

Take, for example, #tlap, the hashtag for Dave Burgess' best-selling book, *Teach Like a PIRATE: Increase Student Engagement, Boost Your Creativity, and Transform Your Life as an Educator*. In its infancy, #tlap was used to exclusively discuss passion-based teaching, but the hashtag has since grown and now touches on other subject areas and topics relevant to educators. And as an added bonus, Burgess frequents the #tlap Twitter chat and adds his insights to the conversation.

Want to start your very own Twitter booktalk? Great! Find a book you are passionate about, create a hashtag, promote your chat through your social media channels and personal connections, set a start date, and Tweet away. Consider discussing one chapter a week so that participants have ample time to participate. During the week, Tweet one question each day using a Q1/A1 format and the chat's hashtag. To spice up your chat, invite the book's author to share insights.

It's not uncommon for online booktalks to take weeks or even months to complete, so consider archiving the conversation using Storify or another service.

What are you waiting for? Start drafting a framework for your very own Twitter booktalk today!

#94 Share Inspirational Quotes on Twitter

Twitter is a great place to find and share daily inspirational quotes. You can create your own image or Retweet an image that somebody has already put out in the Twitter world.

Figure 94-1 is an inspirational quote from *Teach Like a PIRATE* author Dave Burgess.

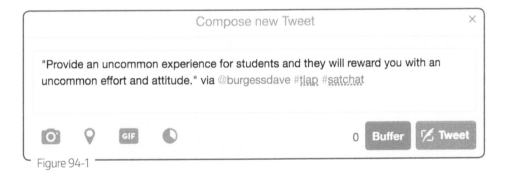

Figure 94-1

#95 Share a Website from Your iPhone

Say, for example, you are on a website like EvolvingEducators.com and you want to share the site with your followers. If you are on an iPhone, simply tap the icon that has a box and arrow pointing upward at the bottom of the screen (Figure 95-1). Once you do this, an option screen will appear (Figure 95-2). From there, tap the Twitter icon and another screen will pop up that will allow you to compose the Tweet. You can also select the account from which you want to Tweet (a personal account or a classroom account, for example). Once you are satisfied with your Tweet, tap *Post*.

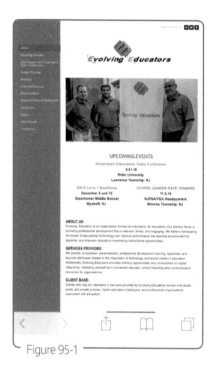
Figure 95-1

Figure 95-2

#96 Visit Cybrary Man's Twitter Page

Cybrary Man (Jerry Blumengarten, aka @cybraryman1) has created a webpage for almost every topic imaginable. Jerry is a retired educator and a current Twitter rock star who consistently contributes to the educational world by archiving relevant content on his website. Make sure you visit his Twitter page (http://cybraryman.com/twitter.html) to learn how to get started on Twitter and participate in a Twitter chat (http://cybraryman.com/howtochat.html).

#97 Learn How Educators Are Using Twitter

Educators across the globe are using Twitter in a myriad of ways. The three of us have used Twitter to join book clubs and grade-specific chats, connect with other schools, and share resources. Some educators are sharing what they do with their students through stories and pictures. Twitter helps educators connect with one another beyond the four walls of their classroom and school building. You can learn more about Twitter by following Pinterest boards or bloggers. The best way to see how educators are using the social media platform, though, is by lurking in the background and watching what they Tweet, how often they Tweet, and with whom they are engaging in the educational world.

#98 Provide Solutions, Rather Than Critiques

When you start to use Twitter regularly and establish yourself through quality Tweets and a solid base of people you follow and your followers, your PLN will call upon you for assistance, help, and feedback. We are in education together, and Twitter provides us all an avenue for assisting each other. The vast majority of educators who use Twitter understand the positive aspects of connecting, sharing, and collaborating and the fact that there is no room for negativity or harsh, unwarranted criticism. Now, this doesn't mean lie if someone asks for your opinion. Rather, we simply encourage you to use Twitter as a means to be a positive influence on education, to help other educators, and to improve our profession.

Section II Conclusion...
You Are a Connected Educator

In Section II, we took the initial skills you learned in Section I and began using them to connect to, learn from, and collaborate with educators around the world. We started building your Twitter stamina, participating in Twitter education chats, learning from conferences you can't attend while making even those conferences you do attend more engaging by using backchannels and meeting your PLN face-to-face. Becoming a connected educator is a commitment, but, we assure you, the rewards are so worth it.

In Section III, you will learn how to become a Twitter rock star.

SECTION 3
BECOMING A
TWITTER ROCK STAR

Congratulations! You are now an active and engaging connected educator who uses Twitter. As you have built your PLN, engaged in Twitter chats, and connected at educational conferences, you have undoubtedly developed a digital footprint, and, along the way, an educational reputation. The next step is to make you a *Twitter rock star*.

The term "Twitter rock star" essentially means you have influence; people look to you for information, advice, and collaboration. But to the three of us, a Twitter rock star is also someone who is an advocate for education and a voice for positive, productive change in the way we teach, students learn, and how we train.

If you initially decided to read this book simply to learn more about Twitter, becoming an advocate on this social media platform may not be your top priority. That's fine. We still encourage you to read Section III, as it outlines the next phase of your Twitter education. However, if you believe being an advocate for education is the natural next step, know that we are so excited and look forward to collaborating with you.

Here we go, future Twitter rock star...

#99 Engage with Thought Leaders

Years ago, it was almost impossible to connect with educational thought leaders. Sure, they wrote their books and spoke at conferences like they do today. But ongoing conversations and one-on-one interactions simply didn't happen on a mass scale outside of those events. Fast-forward to today, and many of those same thought leaders are now on Twitter. And better yet, they're accessible.

Looking to gain insights on effective leadership? Reach out to Todd Whitaker (@ToddWhitaker), a best-selling author who's considered a leading authority on educational leadership. Interested in passion-based teaching and mixing things up in your classroom? Follow *Teach Like a PIRATE* author Dave Burgess (@burgessdave). Is your district or school staff interested in bringing in a speaker who focuses on brain-based learning and intrinsic motivation? Check out *Brain-Powered Strategies to Engage All Learners* author LaVonna Roth (@LaVonnaRoth). Need a Twitter pick-me-up with a few words of encouragement for the day? Look no further than award-winning principal and noted author Salome Thomas-EL (@Principal_EL).

Not only will each of these inspiring educators interact with you on Twitter, but the platform also provides a real-time avenue for them to participate in discussions and positive virtual interactions. So don't be afraid to Tweet these educators asking for help or insights. They are all passionate about helping you and your students grow and succeed. They may even be fans of *your* work and what you share on Twitter. And who knows? You might see them at a conference and be able to grab their attention for a moment because you connected with them on Twitter.

#100 Brand Your Educational Beliefs

All educators have their own educational belief systems. While we may each have different thoughts on exactly how and what to teach, most of us work from a belief system that is student-centered, innovative, and based on pedagogically sound teaching methods. But our methods and ideology shouldn't be set in stone.

Engaging with other connected educators will shape your beliefs and guide your professional growth. As you interact with and learn from other educators, your educational beliefs may be affirmed—or challenged. And that's a good thing! For instance, being exposed to commentary highlighted by hashtags like #youmatter and #ttog (teachers throwing out grades) made us pause to consider a number of viable options for promoting student success.

When you Tweet and Retweet, you are building a brand that's based on your belief system. More importantly, there's a good chance your Tweets will encourage someone who may be struggling to find his or her place as an educator. Your words may be the inspiration another teacher needs to keep going that day.

Keep learning, growing, Tweeting, and inspiring!

#101 Make a Twitter Bulletin Board

You don't need the Internet to reap the benefits of Twitter bulletin boards. A Twitter bulletin board is a space in your classroom where students can show what they know about a particular topic in 140 characters or less (Figure 101-1). Do a Google search for "Twitter bulletin boards," and you will find some pretty cool examples of ways teachers are using these boards in their classrooms to allow students to share their learning and express their ideas.

(Image credit: https://www.pinterest.com/explore/Twitter-board/)

Figure 101-1

One example is in Scott's district, where a first-year geometry teacher put blue paper and the Twitter bird on her door and asked students to post their questions on the door if they did not have a Twitter account. For those who did, she would use Twitter to assist them. However, we can take the concept of Twitter and use it without the technology. You just need to think creatively.

#102 Display a Twitter Feed on a Monitor

A great way to ensure everyone sees your Twitter feed is to display it on a television monitor in a prominent place in your school or classroom. Seeing a Tweet with a picture of a learning or sports activity fosters school pride in teachers and students. Even a simple mention about the school, a class, or individual students' accomplishments displayed on a hallway or cafeteria monitor can help create a positive culture by focusing on what's right at your school. Plus students and teachers alike appreciate being recognized in the virtual world. So why not celebrate their success publically on your school or classroom Twitter feed?

If you need funding for a monitor, ask your Parent Teacher Organization (PTO) or education foundation. Its members may be willing to assist, especially since the monitor will promote student success.

#103 Display Your Twitter Stream with Twitterfall or TweetBeam

Ever wonder how you can effortlessly loop all Tweets that include a specific hashtag on a screen in a class or during an educational event? Twitterfall (Figure 103-1) and TweetBeam (Figures 103-2 and 103-3) are two options that can capture people's Tweets and display them for all to see.

To create your own loop, start by visiting TweetBeam.com or Twitterfall.com. Once you've logged in, search for a hashtag associated with your event and let Tweets start popping up. Then you can push them out through a projector and onto a big screen for the audience's viewing pleasure. It's important to point out that TweetBeam is a paid service, while Twitterfall is free. TweetBeam allows you to filter your search to keep out those pesky and annoying Tweets. Twitterfall allows users to click on and report inappropriate Tweets.

Figure 103-1

Figure 103-2

Figure 103-3

#104 Promote Sharing on Social Media Sites Other Than Twitter

Twitter isn't for everybody. In fact, you might be reading this book thinking Twitter isn't for you, and that's perfectly fine. If nothing else, the one thing we hope you take away from this book is that sharing, both physically and virtually, is important.

If Twitter isn't for you, try a handful of other social media sites, like Pinterest, Facebook, Instagram, Voxer, feedly, and Google+, and see which one you like best. Most people are familiar with Pinterest, Facebook, and Instagram. Voxer and feedly, however, are different animals. Voxer is a tap-to-talk app that allows people to share messages with individuals and groups. Users can listen to the messages in real time or as they wish. Feedly is another app that allows people to save, access, share, and stay current with their favorite websites and blogs. Interestingly, much of what is shared on Twitter is also shared on these other web applications. And just as differentiation is key when trying to meet the needs of diverse learners, one social media platform may work for one connected educator, but not another. Whichever social media site you go with, you will still have access to some of the best professional development in the world.

#105 Manage Your Social Media Accounts with Hootsuite

Hootsuite makes it easy to participate on a variety of social media platforms. Since we're focusing on Twitter, we'll point out that Hootsuite allows you to create multiple columns on one page so you can see your mentions, home page's feed, Retweets, Tweets, direct messages, and more. Hootsuite also allows you to manage your Facebook, Instagram, and Google+ accounts, all in one spot.

#106 Use TweetDeck or Hootsuite for Multiple Chats

TweetDeck (Figure 106-1) and Hootsuite (Figure 106-2) are two easy-to-use apps that can enhance your Twitter experience. Both allow you to have multiple columns pulled up to view a chat and interactions or view several chats at once, but HootSuite works better on a tablet device.

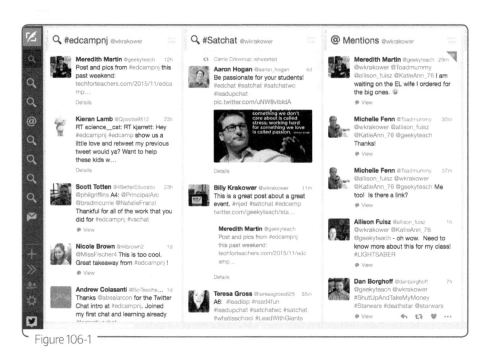

Figure 106-1

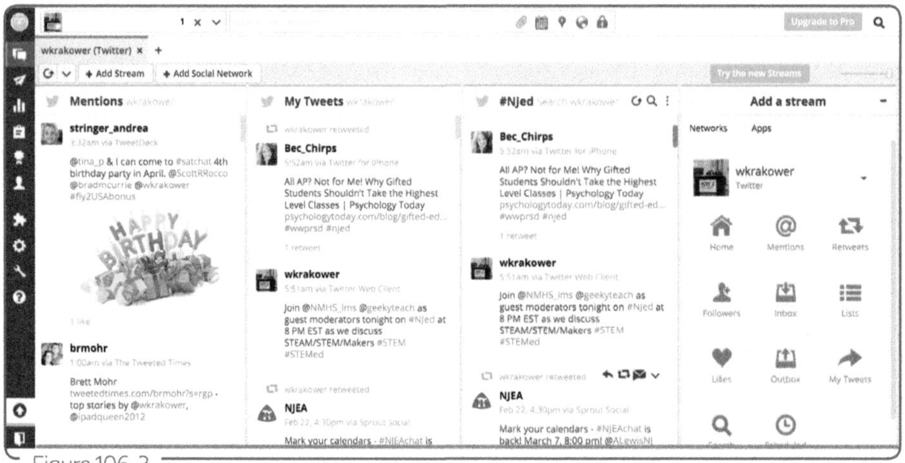

Figure 106-2

#107 Save a Tweet to Pocket

A powerful way to expand your use of Twitter is to use it in conjunction with other apps and online resources. One of our favorites is Pocket, an app that allows you to save something you're interested in so you can view or read it later. We love using Pocket because you never lose an article, research study, image, video, or Tweet. Once you download Pocket from either the App Store or Google Play, the icon (in red in Figure 107-1) shows up below Tweets in your Twitter feed.

Click the Pocket icon under the Tweet you want to save, and it will save it to your Pocket account.

Figure 107-1

#108 Live Stream Events Using Periscope

Are you attending an educational event and want to live stream a favorite speaker for your followers? Download the free Periscope app to your mobile device, register for an account, log in, name the stream, and then Tweet a link to your followers. When they open the link, they'll be able to watch the speaker using any Internet-enabled device. You can use Periscope in any setting, from school events to sports to Edcamps. Educators are now holding virtual workshops on Periscope to share best practices. In Figure 108-1 you can see an "I Have an App for That" session being conducted by the @iteachtvnetwork. Periscope streams can last as long as you like and can be shared privately with specified individuals. Learn more about Periscope at Periscope.tv.

Figure 108-1

#109 Extend a Twitter Chat with Google+, Voxer, and Facebook

Twitter is a great tool for an hour-long discussion on a specific topic. But what if your chat's participants want to continue the conversation after the hour is over? Look no further than Voxer, Facebook, and Google+. These free services can help you extend a Twitter conversation for days, weeks, months, or even years.

Google+ is a platform you can utilize to create communities geared toward a specific topic. For example, you could create a community specifically for a Twitter conversation or hashtag.

Voxer is a tap-to-talk app and web service, with which you can create a group or talk to another person privately. You can access and play "voxes" in real time or at your convenience. A vox is a voice message, picture, text, or video left in the home stream on your Voxer profile page.

Facebook Pages and Groups allow you to build community and keep the conversation going. Given Facebook's popularity, starting either a Page or Group would probably help you promote your Twitter chat well.

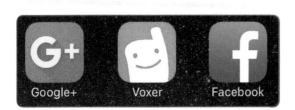

Google+   Voxer   Facebook

If the thought of managing all three platforms and a Twitter chat at once feels overwhelming, choose one to give your Twitter chat an extra boost! Another option would be to use Hootsuite to manage these other applications when looking to extend the Twitter chat.

#110 Schedule Your Tweets Using Buffer

As you use Twitter more and expand your PLN, you will find tons of content you want to share, and sometimes you'll find that content all at once. That's where Buffer comes in.

Instead of posting ten, fifteen, or twenty Tweets in a matter of minutes, use Buffer to space out Tweets so they post throughout the day (Figure 110-1). Through Buffer's website and app, you can schedule up to ten Tweets at once, including event announcements and reminders, as well as interesting articles, preventing you from inundating your PLN with Tweets. Your PLN wants you to contribute, but they don't want you to drown them. Let Buffer help you give your PLN a chance to read what you're posting. Alternatives to Buffer include Hootsuite and TweetDeck, as both have autoscheduling.

Figure 110-1

#111 Vine for Education

As video content continues to gain popularity over images and text, Vine is proving to be a great way to push out small chunks of information. Like Twitter, Vine limits post length, but instead of 140 characters, users have six seconds to make their point. This kind of brevity is something to seriously consider as you try to engage your stakeholders.

Download the Vine app to your smartphone, connect it to your Twitter profile, and share snippets of your classroom, school, or district's story through short bursts of streaming video. Easy to share and fun to watch, Vine is a win-win for everyone.

#112 Share Blogs through feedly

We all have our favorite bloggers, people whose writing inspires us to do bigger and better things. Now, thanks to feedly, you can stay up-to-date on their posts and share them with your followers. Think of this web service as your very own virtual storage facility to house your favorite articles and blog posts.

For example, if you were to add Scott Rocco's *Evolving Educators* blog to your feedly, you would automatically receive updates on the feedly app or website every time he posts. You could then click feedly's Twitter button and share his post with your followers. Looking to download the feedly app? Go into the Apple or Android store, type "feedly" in the search box, and download for free on to your device.

Automatic updates and easy sharing. What could be better?

#113 Create and Share Newsletters and Flyers

If you create digital newsletters or flyers regularly, check out Smore.com When you register for a thirty-day free trial, you can scope out the service's links, texts, images, and catchy templates.

Try it out for yourself. Create a flyer or newsletter using Smore, and then use the service to disseminate your newsletter or promote your event resources across multiple platforms and social media sites, including Twitter. To Tweet your document, simply click Smore's Twitter icon and push it out to your followers. Scott uses Smore for his monthly newsletter to staff. It allows him to

Figure 113-1

bring together the resources he identifies during the month on Twitter and those he saves through Pocket in one location for his staff. He then emails and Tweets out the link. Figure 113-1 is a flyer we created to promote a live #Satchat at ISTE in 2015.

#114 Connect Your Twitter Handle to Your Facebook Page

Managing multiple social media accounts can feel daunting. But if your goal is to connect with the widest possible audience, you'll probably want to be on more than one platform. Luckily, Twitter gives you the option of connecting your account to Facebook. Once you've connected the two, every Tweet you post will show up in your Facebook feed as well. This is a great example of killing two birds with one stone.

Here is a step-by-step process for connecting your accounts through Twitter:

Step 1: Go to Settings on Twitter.

Step 2: Click *Apps*.

Step 3: Select *Connect to Facebook* and provide your Facebook profile information (Figure 114-1).

Figure 114-1

#115 Create a Twitter Recipe with If This Then That

The If This Then That app and web service allows you to create "recipes" by merging two or more web applications to create automatic posts. For example, if you archive your Tweets on Twitter, then they will also go to your Google Drive. Or if you post a photo on Instagram, it will also post to Twitter (Figure 115-1).

Visit IFTTT.com, set up an account, and use the search box to find your favorite Twitter recipe.

Figure 115-1

#116 Tweet from LinkedIn

When it comes to social media, participating on multiple platforms can help you expand your PLN. LinkedIn is definitely one you'll want to consider. Many educators use LinkedIn for professional networking. And since you don't know whether your followers use Twitter or LinkedIn more frequently, you'll want your message to be seen in both places. To address followers on both in one fell swoop, log in to LinkedIn, and go to your home page.

Click the *Share an Update* box, where there is an option to share with the public, just your connections, or the public and Twitter (Figure 116-1). If you select the public and Twitter option, whatever you post to LinkedIn will also be Tweeted to your followers.

Figure 116-1

#117 Use Educational Apps to Make Sharing Easy

The more you use Twitter, the more you will want to use Twitter. The same is true of using web tools designed specifically for social media.

Take, for example, Storify. This savvy web application allows users to archive social media threads, including Twitter. You can archive Twitter chats based on a certain hashtag and push them out to people to view at a later time. When you miss a chat or want to look back on what people posted about a certain topic, Storify helps you catch up.

Simply visit Storify.com and click *Sign up with Twitter* (Figure 117-1). Using Storify to go back in time to relive social media events or access posts is a game-changer and can help make a person's virtual life more efficient. A free alternative to Storify is Participate Learning. It, too, will archive a hashtag discussion on Twitter. Visit https://www.participate.com/chats to access a collection of Tweets associated with a particular educational hashtag such as #Satchat.

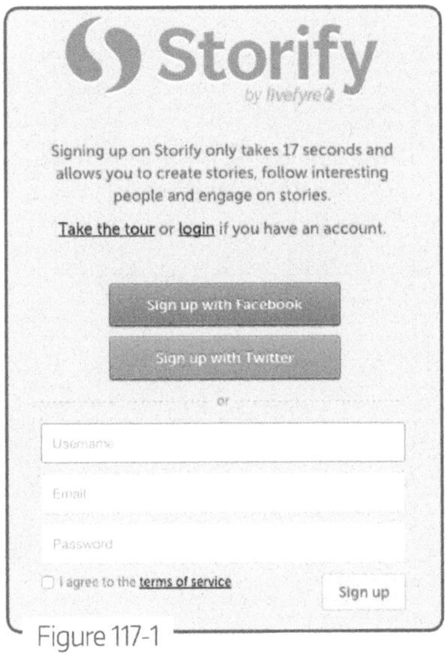

Figure 117-1

#118 Delete Apps Linked to Your Twitter Account

From time to time, you will want to delete an app you registered for using your Twitter handle. Perhaps you no longer use the app or found another app that does the same task better. To delete an app, go to Twitter, then Settings, and click the Apps tab. You will then see all of the apps you have registered for through Twitter. You can revoke an app's access to your account by clicking *Revoke access* (Figure 118-1).

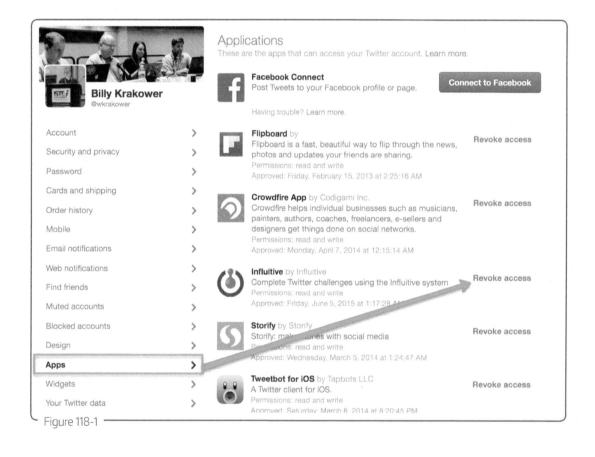

Figure 118-1

#119 Guest Moderate a Chat

Once you've built up your Twitter stamina and reputation, you may feel inclined to guest moderate one of your favorite Twitter chats, or a chat's founder may ask you to guest moderate. Don't sell yourself short; the perspective and experience you bring to the table will prove very beneficial to you as a moderator.

What can you expect when you're asked to guest moderate a Twitter chat?

- Sometimes the chat's founders may pre-select a topic for you, but you should be ready to come up with your own topic.
- Draft eight to ten questions to Tweet during the hour-long discussion. You may not use all of the questions, but it's better to be safe than sorry.
- You may have hundreds of chat participants or just a handful. The day, time, other chats taking place, topic, and additional variables can influence how many people attend your chat. No matter how many people participate, the important thing is to have a meaningful, relevant conversation that ultimately focuses on fostering student success.
- Be prepared to have tough conversations with participants who may not agree with the topic or your questions. It's important to always stay positive when confronted with a negative Tweet.
- Set aside time in the days leading up to the chat to promote it.

#120 Start Your Own Twitter Chat

Chances are that after you guest moderate an education-based Twitter chat, you will want to create your very own.

When thinking about your Twitter chat, one of the first things you will need to do is brainstorm ideas about what your chat will focus on, whether it's a trend, subject, initiative, or stance.

Once you know the topic, you'll need a hashtag to promote your chat. Using the Twitter search feature, try a few relevant words or acronyms to see what's available. Remember that no one owns hashtags, so, theoretically, you could use whatever you want, regardless of who else might be using it. But if you want a hashtag that's exclusive (not being used for purposes other than your chat), come up with something unique. For example, if you wanted to focus on high school, see if "#hschat" or "#highschoolchat" is available. You'll want to use that hashtag when you promote, run, and archive your chat.

Next, you will need to figure out a day and time to hold your chat. In the past few years, educational chats have flooded the Twitter world, so it's likely there will be another chat going on the same time as the one you created. Remember to pick a time that encompasses the most time zones as well. For example, if you want to host a chat open to all educators in the United States, you do not want to have your hour-long chat at 4 p.m. (ET), because people on the West Coast will still be in school. It's important to promote your chat not only on Twitter, but also on other social media outlets in the days leading up to it.

During the chat, Tweet and Retweet your questions to keep participants focused. You'll also need to Retweet and comment on participants' answers and insights to maintain a forward momentum. Remember to use the Q1/A1 format to keep the conversation organized. You may also consider recruiting a few moderators to support you and help you run the chat. Once your chat is complete, archive it so that people can go back and read the Tweets. As discussed earlier, a great tool to use for archiving purposes is Participate Learning. Visit https://www.participate.com/chats and locate the hashtag that you are interested in archiving. Don't see it? No problem. Reach out to their customer service department and they will add your hashtag to their database. Once the hashtag is archived for the time period selected, you can then push it out for all the world to see.

If you are committed and passionate about your Twitter chat, it will ultimately be successful and help move the conversation about your chosen topic forward.

#121 Keep These Twitter Chat Tools On Hand

Tool	Website/App	Purpose
Facebook	Facebook.com	Bring attention to your Twitter chat and provide participants with reminders, archives, and other important information pertaining to the chat through Facebook.
Google Sheets	Google.com/drive/	Use Google Sheets to help organize weekly topics, questions, and guest moderators.
Smore	Smore.com	Promote your Twitter chat using a digital newsletter. Smore allows users to upload text, images, links, and so much more.

Tool	Website/App	Purpose
Storify	Storify.com	Archive your Twitter chat with Storify. Make sure to do it right after your chat ends so it's easier for you to manage.
Voxer	Voxer.com	Extend your hour-long Twitter chat discussion with Voxer. This tap-to-talk web application is very beneficial for educators. Create a group for your Twitter chat participants so they can leave messages about the topic.

#122 Make the Trending List

Once you have co-moderated a chat and maybe even formed your own chat, it's time to find out if you are having an effect on education through Twitter. For many of us, this means our hashtag making the trending list. Though this shouldn't be your only metric of success, let's be honest, making the list is a very cool feeling. Engagement is another way you can tell if a hashtag or chat is having an impact. The number of Retweets, replies, and likes helps with unofficially determining how successful something is on Twitter. Sites like Storify and Participate Learning can help you determine how many Tweets took place during a given time period.

Landing on Twitter's trending list is an interesting process, but the bottom line is that the more a hashtag is Tweeted in a short amount of time, the more likely it is to trend. You can find the trending list on the left-hand side of your Twitter page.

What you may not know, however, is that you can see what's trending in a specific geographic area. In Figure 122-1, we have United States trends. But you can also choose to see trends in a specific area. Just click *Change* in the top right-hand corner, and you will see the menu in Figure 122-2.

Figure 122-1

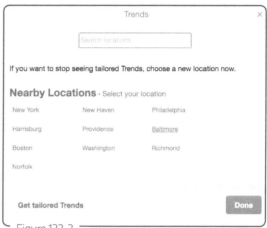

Figure 122-2

Choose the city or type in a location to find out the trending hashtags and topics for that area. Or you could take your curiosity to another level by clicking *Get tailored Trends*. What are tailored trends? Well, below is a description from Twitter on what it does (Figure 122-3). A simpler way of describing tailored trends is that it helps the Twitter user find local trends that are new or emerging in your area. If you don't like your tailored trends, click *Change*, and you can go back to viewing trends in other locations.

Figure 122-3

It takes a while to make the trending list, but when you do...it is really a cool feeling. Happy trending!

#123 Add Your Twitter Chat to a Global Calendar

Several years ago, there were very few Twitter chats, but today, these virtual discussions are taking the educational world by storm. At any given time, you can take your pick of Twitter chats: #Satchat, #tlap, #edtechchat, #whatisschool, #SatchatOZ, #SatchatWC, #SatchatME, and hundreds more, giving Twitter users a plethora of options for expanding their PLN.

To help your Twitter chat gain visibility and become better known in the virtual world, add it to the global calendar of educational chats (https://sites.google.com/site/Twittereducationchats/home). While you're there, browse the chats by day or hashtag.

#124 Use Google Sheet Script to Archive Twitter Chat

When it comes time to archive your Twitter chat, you have a number of options for archival services. What does it mean to archive in relation to Twitter? In simple terms, it means that a user is grouping selected Tweets based on a specific hashtag or topic. Storify is a simple solution; however, keep in mind that Storify and other services may limit the number of Tweets you can archive. Google Sheet Script, such as TAGS, is a little more complex, but allows you to create a larger archive. TAGS is free, and once you watch the video tutorial (https://tags.hawksey.info/), it's easy to use.

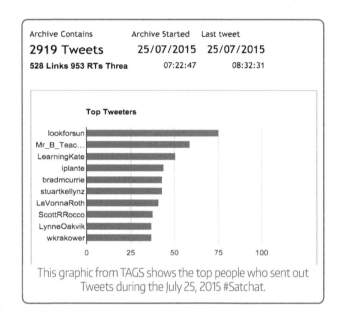

Figure 124-1 shows another format for tracking statistics for a chat using a Google Sheet Script. The stats shown are from a #Satchat live we did at the ASCD L2L Conference in July 2015. It shows the number of Tweets each person sent out, along with the number of @ mentions each person got, and how many RTs (Retweets) were sent. It also displays the number of Tweets that occurred in that period along with a rate per minute. You can also click on the blue link next to each person's Twitter handle to see what they Tweeted during that particular chat.

This graphic from TAGS shows the top people who sent out Tweets during the July 25, 2015 #Satchat.

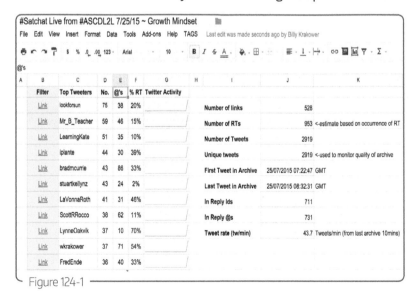

Figure 124-1

#125 Archive a Hashtag Using Storify

The growing popularity of Twitter chats and use of hashtags at events has created the need to archive these virtual conversations. One way to archive a hashtag on Twitter is to use Storify. To get started, visit Storify.com and register for a free account. Once you've registered and logged in, type the hashtag you want to archive and, presto, Tweets with that hashtag will pop up in a stream.

The ability to go back and pull Tweets that have a specific hashtag is a pretty neat feature and gives your chat's fans or a conference's participants the opportunity to learn even after the event. Once you have created your archive on Storify, you have the option to share it via social media (Figure 125-1). Select the option that best suits your sharing needs. Archives can also provide educators with a resource to springboard off of when trying out new tools or methods in school. For example, if you participated in a #Satchat discussion that focused on Google Apps for Education and wanted to show examples to your colleagues of what was discussed, you could provide them with a link from Storify pertaining to that specific Twitter conversation.

Figure 125-1

#126 Track Your Twitter Analytics

As you develop your social media presence, you will want to know if you are having an effect in the educational world. Fortunately, Twitter provides you a set of analytics to determine how influential your Tweets are within the Twitterverse.

Figure 126-1

Take, for example, Scott's pinned Tweet in Figure 126-1.

Click the bars icon (Figure 126-1), and you will see a chart similar to Figure 126-2 outlining that Tweet's activity—the number of total impressions (how many times people saw the Tweet) and how many times people engaged or interacted with the Tweet by liking, Retweeting, clicking, or replying.

This gives you an idea of your Tweet's impressions and total engagement. Not happy with your engagement stats on Twitter? Continue to play around with embedding relevant hashtags like #GoogleEdu or #Edtech in your Tweets. Often people search for hashtags on Twitter when trying to find information about a specific topic, such as Google Apps for Education via the #GoogleEdu hashtag. Note: A pinned Tweet will most likely have more impressions and more total engagements than your other Tweets because it's always at the top of your feed.

Analytics become an important part of your presence on social media as you become an established, connected educator. The simple fact here is that as Twitter becomes more a part of your daily routine, you want to have more of a sense of the impact your Tweets are having on your followers. When you are looking for content to Tweet, consider your Twitter followers' needs and interests. Tweets that are inspirational, informative, or relevant earn the most Retweets.

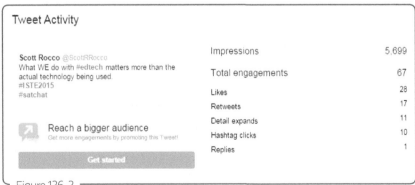

Figure 126-2

#127 The Education World Needs You! (by Dave Burgess)

To thrive on Twitter and to use this game-changing platform to positively impact the educational landscape, educators must overcome two primary obstacles.

The first is the belief that their ideas are either not worthy of sharing or not unique enough to warrant adding into the conversation. This is a false belief! You have amazing ideas and experiences that are unique to you and your path as an educator. And what you have to add to the conversation may be exactly what someone needs to hear. Share everything! The things that were successful as well as all the stuff that didn't work! You may help others—or save them from making the mistakes you've made.

I constantly hear teachers say, "I'm sure everyone does this." No! They don't! Even if your idea is not new, you have probably put a personalized spin on it. Others can build on your idea to create something powerful for themselves. Furthermore, if you share something in a chat that others already know or do, that doesn't annoy people; it validates their practices and experiences. By talking about an idea they're trying to implement, you reinforce their belief in the soundness of the practice. You'll also encourage those who may be under fire for trying something innovative. Hearing about your experiences raises their confidence and enables them to continue to fight the good fight.

The second obstacle is the insidious belief that sharing your thoughts, ideas, and what has been successful for you is somehow selfish or egotistical. Nothing could be further from the truth! As Don Wettrick wrote in *Pure Genius*, "If you have found something that works, share that knowledge with the educational community. It isn't bragging, it's helping."

The vast majority of educators on Twitter go there to collaborate, share, and support fellow educators with the ultimate goal of making school a more empowering place for all. We don't just want you to share your amazing work—we need you to share it. It is, in fact, your responsibility to share what you know that could help others.

There is nothing selfish or egotistical about becoming a valuable member of the educational Twittersphere. If a person collapsed at a crowded party and stopped breathing and you knew CPR, would it be selfish to let it be known loudly and in no uncertain terms that you could help? Of course not! Would anybody think you were being egotistical if you even aggressively pushed your way to the front in order to save the victim? No way! You would be celebrated as a hero.

Our purpose as educators is just as mighty! We change lives. We literally save lives. We need your contributions. We need you to share your special perspective and to add your voice to this ongoing discussion centered on transforming the world into a better place. We are so glad you're here!

#128 Start an Educational Movement

What is it that you are passionate about in education? What practices do you want to innovate or improve? By harnessing the power of social media, you can make a powerful, positive difference in both the virtual world and the *real* world. Start by getting really clear about your message—the problem you want to address and the solution you want people to consider. Then come up with a catchy, short hashtag to symbolize your movement. Next, start Tweeting your thoughts using your new hashtag. Over time, your message and hashtag will inspire other educators, who will then share the love through their own social media channels. Check out these exemplars: #COLchat, #ttog, #EDBeat, and #digilead.

Scott went through this exact process when he started his educational movement, #ASuperDay. Read his blog post (found at http://bit.ly/18hkTP6) leading up to the first #ASuperDay chat:

Great things happen in our classrooms, schools, and school districts. Each day, teachers and students come together with the common goal of learning. Building principals and subject supervisors lead instruction, professional development trainings, and building-level activities. Office personnel, custodial and maintenance staff, classroom aides, and educational support personnel provide valued services and support to the facilities and educational organization. Classrooms, schools, school districts, and those who work in them are part of a complex educational system that has more things going on in a day than can be explained.

But over the last few years, as a connected educator through Twitter and other social media resources, I have read and viewed posts, blogs, and videos about the activities that happen in this complex educational system. I've also seen educators in classrooms and school offices describe what their days are like, what they do in a given day, and the activities they participate in based on their responsibilities in a school district. These windows into the life of a principal, teacher, or supervisor are enlightening, engaging, and positive examples of the great things happening in education today.

But friends and people outside of education often ask me what I do each day as a superintendent of schools. They want to know what life is like as a superintendent; what does a "regular" day involve? Then, recently, I followed Tweets from principals using #APrincipalDay. It was fascinating and wonderful to read what principals across the country were doing on this one day. Following the hashtag brought me back to my days as an elementary school principal. But more importantly, the day highlighted the important things principals do during their daily routine as the educational leaders of their buildings.

That was the ah-ha moment for me: why not have a similar day with superintendents from around the country Tweeting about their day, their activities, and experiences with a common hashtag? But what should we call the day? That's when I reached out to Michael Lubelfeld (@mikelubelfeld) and Nick Polyak (@npolyak), two fellow connected educators and superintendents, about the concept. I threw out a few hashtag ideas, but the one I thought would be best was ***#ASuperDay***. Think about it: Great things happen each day in our schools, and superintendents are part of those great things as the educational leaders of their school districts. Therefore, these days are super days!

#129 Host a Social Media Lounge

By this point, we hope you find value in using social media for personal and professional development and for sharing meaningful ideas. And we hope you'll advocate for its use among educators.

One way you can help promote the positive use of social media in education is by developing and hosting a social media lounge at local, state, and national conferences. A social media lounge is an informal gathering of educators that network in a certain area at educational events. Often they will share ideas and help people become connected and see the benefits of social media in education. If you are connected to a conference through one of your professional organizations, suggest the idea; and even if you aren't an official member, suggest the idea to an organization hosting a conference.

Brad and Scott, along with two awesome connected New Jersey principals, Dr. Spike Cook (@DrSpikeCook) and Stephen Santilli (@SPSantilli), had the opportunity to run a social media lounge at the 2015 conference for the New Jersey Principals and Supervisors Association and the New Jersey Association of School Curriculum Development. The information below was posted in that event's guide. From it, you can see a few of the topics we covered. As you prepare to host a social media lounge at an event, consider addressing questions you hear from teachers in your school or district about how to make the most of social media.

» Social Media Lounge – Twitter 101 and 201 **Room: Promenade 7/8**

Brad Currie, Supervisor of Instruction, Chester School District; Spike Cook, Principal, Millville Public Schools; Steve Santilli, Principal, Hamilton Township School District; Scott Rocco, Superintendent, Spotswood Public Schools
Learn all about social media in an informal environment. During each session there will be an opportunity to focus on various aspects of social media. This session will address:
-Twitter 101: The basics of Twitter and how it can enhance your professional growth.
-Twitter 201: Follow a step-by-step plan on how to fully utilize all that Twitter has to offer.

» Social Media Lounge – Tap to Talk PD with Voxer and Online Book Talks Via Edmodo**Room: Promenade 7/8**

Brad Currie, Supervisor of Instruction, Chester School District; Spike Cook, Principal, Millville Public
Learn all about social media in an informal environment. During each session there will be an opportunity to focus on various aspects of social media. This session will address:
Tap to Talk PD with Your VOXER: Participants will learn how to utilize the Voxer app on their Device to connect and share.
Online Book Talks via Edmodo: Read a book and hold a virtual conversation with staff using Edmodo.

» Social Media Lounge – Leveraging the Power of Blogs – Tell Your Story **Room: Promenade 7/8**

Brad Currie, Supervisor of Instruction, Chester School District; Spike Cook, Principal, Millville Public Schools; Steve Santilli, Principal, Hamilton Township School District; Scott Rocco, Superintendent, Spotswood Public Schools
Learn all about social media in an informal environment. During each session there will be an opportunity to focus on various aspects of social media. This session will address:
Leveraging the Power of Blogs: Participants will learn about the power of reading and writing blogs to enhance reflection and stay on top of best practices in the field of education.
Tell Your Story: Learn how web tools such as Twitter, Facebook, Instagram, Pinterest, YouTube, iMovie and Animoto can help schools connect with stakeholders.

» Social Media Lounge – Web Tools to Enhance Communication and Collaboration – What's on My iPad? **Room: Promenade 7/8**

Brad Currie, Supervisor of Instruction, Chester School District; Spike Cook, Principal, Millville Public Schools; Steve Santilli, Principal, Hamilton Township School District; Scott Rocco, Superintendent, Spotswood Public Schools
Learn all about social media in an informal environment. During each session there will be an opportunity to focus on critical aspects of social media. This session will address:
-Web Tools to Enhance Communication and Collaboration: Participants will learn about Google Apps, Remind 101, SW911, Podcasting, Google Hangouts and Push to Talk Apps to communicate and collaborate with stake holders.
-What's on my iPad/Chromebook? Participants will gain exposure to 20 best practice apps that can be used instantly in the school setting.

#130 Turn Your Twitter Chat into a Radio Show

Twitter chats have led to dozens of educational podcasts and radio shows, each providing moderators the opportunity to extend the conversation and bring in experts. Once your Twitter chat has gained popularity, it might be a good idea to extend those conversations into an online radio show or podcast. Platforms like Garage Band, SoundCloud, or Audacity allow you to record your show. Alternatively, you can record a Skype session or conduct a Google Hangout On Air. Both Skype and Google Hangout On Air are free and can be accomplished with a few clicks of the mouse. If you don't already have one, you'll also need to purchase a microphone that can connect to your computer for recording purposes.

The show itself should only be about ten minutes in length. Sometimes the moderators of the chat just record themselves talking about topics, and other times they will bring on a guest. The recording can then be digitized and shared on the Internet.

EdtechChat Radio is an example of how a weekly Twitter chat discussion can turn into a very successful radio show. Sharon Plante, Susan Bearden, Alex Podchaski, and Tom Murray moderate #EdtechChat every Monday night at eight (ET). Various topics pertaining to educational technology are discussed. Often guest moderators will participate in the Twitter chat and then be interviewed on the radio show. The show can be found by visiting this website: http://www.bamradionetwork.com/edtechchat/.

Teach Cow (@TeachCow) is a great example of a podcast and Twitter radio show. Check out the shows at TeachCow.com or by searching for *Teachers Talk Live* on iTunes. The podcast's founder, Dr. Greg Goins (@wfsuper), is doing some amazing things and providing great content based on Twitter.

#131 Participate in Connect an Educator Day

Each year on May 2, Connect an Educator Day, we work with other connected educators to demonstrate the power of social media in education and help those who have yet to connect.

Scott wrote the following blog post on our first Connect an Educator Day.

The days and times are consistent, but the topics vary. On any given day, at any particular time, you can find educators coming together for a discussion on a topic related to their subject area, students, or profession. These discussions happen on Twitter, Google Communities, Voxer, and other social media platforms. However, have you ever wondered what percentage of educators use social media? The ones who do use it are called "connected educators." I have no statistics on this, but believe the actual percentage, compared to the total number of educators in the world, is probably low.

Thinking back to when I started using social media, I did not know where to begin, who to follow, or how to connect. Since those first days in 2012, I've figured it out along the way. For me, and many connected educators, the opportunity to connect provides great professional value. The mere fact that I can simply jump on the social media platform of my choice and immediately connect to, learn from, and collaborate with other educators based on an interest is simply amazing.

Over the years, many connected educators have made an effort to help connect those who are not connected. In a recent #Satchat discussion, we discussed the topic "To Connect or Not Connect?" During that discussion, I heard so many great ideas about why educators should connect, the value of being a connected educator, and how to use these professional connections to improve ourselves. During the discussion, our #Satchat team, me (@ScottRRocco), Brad Currie (@BradMCurrie), and Billy Krakower (@wkrakower), launched our next effort to help colleagues: Connect an Educator Day.

The purpose of this day will be for connected educators to help a colleague who is not connected to social media as a means of professional and personal development connect on May 2, 2015. For those looking to participate, here is how it will work:

Prior to May 2, 2015:

Model and demonstrate the value of being a connected educator with colleagues who are not connected.

Encourage educators not connected to start a social media account.

Show educators not connected what is available to them when they connect (resources, information, colleagues, etc.).

On May 2, 2015:

Have them join (and you, too) #Satchat at 7:30 a.m. (ET) for Connect an Educator Day.

#Satchat will lower the total number of questions to four during the chat to slow down the discussion and encourage the newly connected educators to participate.

Resources, links, videos, and other information will be provided to the newly connected educators participating.

Connect an Educator Day is designed to encourage those who have yet to connect to social media to do so—with the help of you, the connected educator.

What about you? Will you help an educator connect? Will you be part of Connect an Educator Day on May 2? The next stage of being a connected educator is participating in activities and events that promote the positive use of social media by educators that encourages their participation.

#132 Add a Twitter Poll

Sometimes you want your PLN's opinion. Or maybe your class needs to collect data for a social studies research project. In either case, a poll may be the tool you need for the job. And thanks to a great new Twitter feature, you can embed a poll in your Tweet.

Figure 132-1

For example, during the #Satchat on November 14, 2015, the conversation topic was "Voice in Education." Brad posted a poll for our PLN to respond to during the discussion (Figure 132-1).

Chat participants taking part in the poll selected their choice and then clicked *Vote* (Figure 132-2).

Figure 132-2

Once their vote was cast, the poll taker instantly saw the poll results (Figure 132-3).

They could then return to the poll later on to see updated results (Figure 132-4).

Once the poll closed twenty-four hours later, it looked like Figure 132-5.

To create a Twitter poll of your own:

Step 1: Click the compose Tweet icon in the upper right-hand corner of your screen.

Step 2: Click the poll icon at the bottom of your Compose new Tweet box.

Step 3: Write your question, add your options, and then Tweet out your poll for the world to see (Figure 132-6).

Figure 132-3

Figure 132-4

Figure 132-6

Figure 132-5

#133 Crowdsource Using Google Apps

As fellow education advocates, we know that, like us, you want to create and provide valuable resources for your PLN. One way we do this for our PLNs is by crowdsourcing during #Satchat using Google Docs, Slides, and Sheets. Crowdsourcing is when people can contribute to

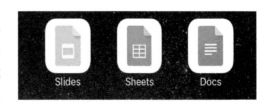

a live digital product in real time or at their leisure. Part of the Google Apps for Education portfolio, Docs, Slides, and Sheets allow multiple users to collaborate in real time.

Say you want to put together a list of apps or websites that address the Substitution, Augmentation, Modification, and Redefinition (SAMR) Model. Simply create a Google Doc, Slide, or Sheet, and set your share settings to *public*. Then copy the link and Tweet it to your followers so they can access it.

During a #Satchat discussion, participants collaborated to compile a list of education apps they like. We titled the Google Sheet "60 Apps in 60 Minutes" (Figure 133-1). When the chat concluded, we made sure the participants—and all our followers—had access to the final sheet by sending out a link. We also posted the link so that anyone who visits our site can download it.

60 Apps in 60 Minutes			
#Satchat PLN Generated List from 09-19-2015 Twitter Chat			
Name of App	**Who is it for (student, parent, teacher, professional learning, etc.)**	**How do you use it/ What does it do?**	**Where can you find it?**
Plickers	Teacher/students	For assessing questions, quizzes, collating answers	the app store @plickers
Quizlet	Students, Teachers	Interactive Vocabulary app, flashcards, games, tests	app store
Kahoot	Students	Gamify assessment	online: getkahoot.com
TodaysMeet	Students/teachers	backchanneling conversation	online: todaysmeet.com
Quiver	Students	motivation. fun.	@quivervision android/ios
Seesaw	Student/Teacher/Parent	assessing, comprehension, fluency, everything. Students can video, pics, voice, draw	http://web.seesaw.me/
Kidblog	Student, Teacher	Blogging, global connections	
ClassCraft	Class	turns entire class into game environment - levels, powers, rewards and incentives	http://www.classcraft.com/
Poll Everywhere	Student/Teacher/Parent/ColleaguePD	Standalone polling/response or responses within Keynote/PowerPoint presentations	https://www.polleverywhere.com/
Padlet	Student/teachet	Collaborative sticky notes	Padlet.com
EdPuzzle	Teacher/students	Instruction (flipping), assessment (formative)	http://edpuzzle.com
Green Screen Doink	Students/Teachers	Allows easy to use green screen in photos/videos or both	app store
Remind	Students/teachers	Can send text messages to classes or sports teams. I use it for faculty messages	Remind.com
@goformative	Students	quick assessments, open response allows to show work	https://goformative.com/
Jeopardy	Students	create easy jeopardy games	https://www.jeopardy.rocks/signUp
Vocaroo	students, teachers	students quickly record voice; read story; respond;	http://vocaroo.com/

Figure 133-1

#134 Connect with Colleges and Universities

Finally, being an advocate for education means that you expand your PLN to include higher-level organizations, specifically universities and colleges. Higher education institutions around the world are taking to Twitter to tell their stories, particularly education departments.

From a professional development standpoint, it makes sense for a school of education to have its own Twitter handle. The school of education can share resources and information with pre-service teachers, which, coincidentally, works in the soon-to-be teachers' favor, since most of them already expect to communicate through social media. For example, the Rider School of Education pushes out content from their Twitter handle related to best practices in education. Students in this program follow the department on Twitter to stay current with educational resources.

A Twitter handle can also help colleges and universities virtually engage current students and graduates. Alumni especially take pride knowing their college is well-represented and continuing to do great things. A social media presence doesn't hurt in the recruiting arena, either. What's one of the first things families do when researching a school? They go to Facebook and Twitter. A higher education institution's virtual reputation is just as important as its physical one.

The bottom line is this: The more we model appropriate use of social media, the more likely students (even in higher education) will follow suit.

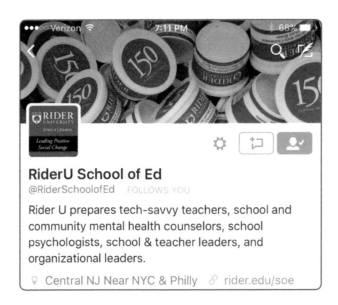

#135 Take Advantage of the Opportunities Twitter Offers Educators

As you start to provide and consume information through Twitter, you will begin to collaborate with other connected educators, opportunities you wouldn't have had if you weren't a connected educator.

For the three of us, these opportunities have included:

- Guest moderating Twitter chats from around the globe
- Collaborating on educational projects
- Critiquing educational technology
- Presenting at conferences inside and outside our home state
- Writing portions for others' books
- Authoring books—like this one!

Opportunities abound for connected educators who collaborate through Twitter. In fact, at some point, you may have to decide how involved you really want to be. We'll provide you with suggestions on how you can get involved, but don't limit yourself to our examples. Forge your own path and develop new ways for educators to use Twitter. In the pages that follow, you'll read about experiences that have been positive for us, and that we hope will prove positive for you, too.

#136 Brand Your Education Business

As you become a more established, connected educator who has a clear view of your profession, you'll find that people will want to hear what you have to say. They may ask you to speak at a conference, write an article or blog post, evaluate a product, or consult on a project. Not only is this exciting, but it also means you may have a budding business, all because of your first Tweet and each one that followed.

Differentiate your message and take your business to the next level by giving it a Twitter presence. You could even create your own hashtag to tag your Tweets with. When setting up your profile, include a profile picture, cover photo, a short description of your business, and a link to your company's website, if you have one. Push out a mix of business-related Tweets and resources daily, each time including relevant hashtags to get more exposure for your message. Because of the prevalent use of social media apps on mobile devices, you will be able to meet prospective clients wherever they are.

#137 Tweet Feedback to Education Companies

Thanks to Twitter, you can now provide feedback directly to the companies creating the educational products you use all the time. You'll find that education companies are always looking for ways to improve their products. Twitter gives you a convenient way to share your insights with them.

To ask a company questions or make recommendations for one of its products, include its Twitter handle as well as a relevant hashtag. Doing so increases the likelihood that your Tweet gets noticed. Also, be polite and respectful. Most of the time the company will reply, and it may let you know that advice you've given is already being addressed. And who knows? The company might even send you some swag for the great feedback.

Check out Figure 137-1 and a Tweet Brad Currie addressed to Remind, which is a wonderful and free communication tool that schools use to push out content to stakeholders via text, email, or push notifications on apps. Visit Remind.com for more details.

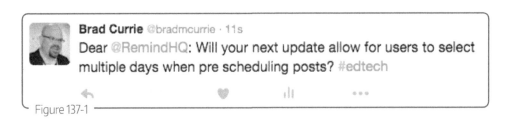

Figure 137-1

#138 Purchase a Twitter Ad

If you have a few extra bucks lying around the house that could be spent on promoting your company or cause, give Twitter ads a try.

To purchase an ad, go to the area on your home page near your profile pic in the upper right-hand corner of your screen and click *Twitter Ads*. From there, you will be taken to a website that will ask you to set up a new campaign, select an audience, set a budget, and select options to make your campaign Tweets unique.

Purchasing Twitter ads is a great opportunity to highlight an event, book, or product. You never know the effect an ad could have on your followers.

#139 Just Be You!

Tweet about what you believe in. Tweet about how educators can come together, how we can improve, and about how we can promote the success of students. Tweet often and Tweet with passion! Above all, be authentic. Authenticity rules on Twitter.

But while you're "just being honest," remember that if your Tweets come off as negative, overly critical, or focused on your personal agenda, you are probably wasting your time—and others' time. Instead, share resources that can ultimately have a positive impact on the world of education.

Be daring and take risks with Twitter to start new conversations. Being a connected educator on Twitter provides so many opportunities to change the educational conversation and move everyone forward in a positive direction.

Tweeting is all about passion, brevity, reflection, sharing, and most importantly learning. Use this magnificent tool to grow as an educator. The more you grow the better chance there is to help other like-minded educators and help students become the best they can possibly be.

Don't worry about knowing all the answers or having the right title behind your name. Share generously. Be authentic. Chat honestly about what needs to change and about what's working well. Just be yourself because, as the saying goes, everyone else is already taken.

#140 The History of #Satchat

Our story has very humble beginnings. The three of us didn't start Twitter accounts with a specific purpose or goal in mind. It was 2012 and, in all honesty, we weren't sure if Twitter was a flash-in-the-pan technology, or something without any educational value that we wouldn't really use. All we had was an idea for a little chat that would promote a productive and positive educational conversation between educators. Oh, how naïve we were!

Scott Rocco and Brad Currie felt there was an opportunity for educational leaders in the classroom, school, and district to collaborate, share, and reflect informally in the virtual world. Both were new to the world of Twitter and wanted to take full advantage of all it had to offer in terms of helping them grow professionally. Scott reached out to Brad via direct message about moderating an educational Twitter chat. They bounced around a few ideas and decided to focus on coming up with a chat aimed at classroom, school, and district leaders. Finding the right day and time would be the next crucial step. Given that most educators were off on Saturdays and that early in the morning would be a somewhat quiet time, we chose 7:30–8:30 a.m. (ET). Thus, #Satchat was born.

Scott and Brad hosted the first #Satchat April 14, 2012; Billy Krakower joined the team that summer. The first-ever #Satchat Live was held in October 2012 at the EdScape Conference. #Satchat Live is often held at educational events like the NASSP Ignite Conference and EdCampNJ. Scott, Billy, and Brad will moderate #Satchat in front of a live audience and bring on special guests to discuss topics. It's also recorded on Google Hangouts so that people can watch on their computers from home.

In its infancy, #Satchat averaged around twenty or twenty-five participants a week. Fast-forward to today, and it has exploded, with about 400 people participating each week. In fact, #Satchat hit the 600-participant mark for the first time during the 2015 season and an all-time high of over 700 participants later in 2015.

In 2013, #Satchat expanded its influence to the West Coast using the #SatchatWC hashtag with Shelley Burgess, David Culberhouse, and Darin Jolly co-moderating the conversation. In the past few years, the #Satchat family has expanded even more with the additions of #SatchatOZ (Australia), #SatchatME (Middle East), Satchat Voxer, Satchat Radio, and Satchat Live. With the help of people from around the world like Andrea Stringer, Holly Fairbrother, Sarah Thomas, Justin Schleider, and Ashley Hurley, #Satchat is helping move the conversation forward. Additionally, connecting with inspiring educators the likes of Eric Sheninger, Vicki Davis, Todd Whitaker, and Salome Thomas-EL, among others, brings a sense of community to the chat and has been an added benefit of having a Twitter- and hashtag-based conversation.

Though the chat has grown considerably over the years, one thing remains the same. Each and every week, #Satchat provides current and emerging school leaders the opportunity to share their insights on topics ranging from technology integration, social media, and professional development to crisis management, vision, bullying, leadership, and teacher recruitment. Educators can instantly turn these ideas into practices that can have a profound effect on a wide array of school stakeholders. For example, during a recent #Satchat conversation, someone mentioned that they were embedding a student Edcamp into the weekly schedule. Several school leaders participating in #Satchat, including Brad, began to then think about how this could be done in his own school. It is this remarkable camaraderie among participants that has made #Satchat a true example of collaboration.

And since the chat primarily takes place on Twitter, each and every participant has a voice, the chance to collaborate all day, every day, and the opportunity to experience for themselves the value of using Web 2.0 tools in an educational setting.

We're excited about what the future holds for #Satchat. The entire #Satchat family is very proud of all that our chat has done (and will continue to do) for educators. We believe, though, that #Satchat is just one example of how educators regularly go above and beyond the call of duty to better themselves professionally so they can promote student success.

Now, how will Twitter affect your professional life and development? How will you use Twitter to improve your craft and promote the success of students? We hope you'll use Twitter to get connected, grow, learn, and to help others by sharing your ideas. What are you waiting for? The world needs your voice!

Resources

Apps

Audacity - AudacityTeam.org

Buffer - BufferApp.com

Canva - Canva.com

Crowdfire - CrowdfireApp.com

Feedly – Feedly.com

GarageBand – available on iTunes

Google Docs – Google.com/docs/about

Google Hangouts – Hangouts.google.com

Google Hangout On Air – Gangouts.google.com/onair

Google Sheet Script - Developers.google.com/apps-script and Tags.hawksey.info

Google Sheets – Google.com/sheets/about

Google Slides – Google.com/slides/about

Google URL Shortener – Goo.gl

Hootsuite – Hootsuite.com

If This Then That – Ifttt.com/recipes

InstaQuote – available on iTunes

Participate Learning – Participate.com

Periscope – Periscope.tv

Pocket – GetPocket.com

Remind – Remind.com

Smore – Smore.com

SoundCloud – SoundCloud.com

Storify – Storify.com

Tagboard – Tagboard.com

TweetDeck – TweetDeck.twitter.com

TwitterBeam – TwitterBeam.com

Twitterfall – TwitterFall.com

Vine – Vine.co

Voxer – Voxer.com

Blogs

BillyKrakower.com

Bradcurrie.net

EvolvingEducators.wordpress.com

Books

Jason Bretzmann et al. – *Personalized PD: Flipping Your Professional Development*

Dave Burgess – *Teach Like a PIRATE: Increase Student Engagement, Boost Your Creativity, and Transform Your Life as an Educator*

Brad Currie – *All Hands on Deck: Tools for Connecting Parents, Educators, and Communities*

Billy Krakower – *Connecting Your Students to the World: Tools and Projects to Make Global Collaboration Come Alive, K-8*; *Using Technology to Engage Students with Disabilities*

LaVonna Roth – *Brain-Powered Strategies to Engage All Learners*

Eric Sheninger – *Digital Leadership: Changing Paradigms for Changing Times*

Don Wettrick – *Pure Genius: Building a Culture of Innovation and Taking 20% Time to the Next Level*

Other Resources

Cybrary Man's Twitter chat calendar – cybraryman.com/chats.html

EdTechchat Radio – bamradionetwork.com/edtechchat

Education Twitter chat list – https://sites.google.com/site/Twittereducationchats

TeachCow.com

Twitter Chats & Hashtags

#140EduTips – *140 Twitter Tips for Educators*

#4thchat – Fourth-grade teachers

#APrincipalDay – Principals chat

#ArkEdChat – Arkansas education

#ASuperDay – Superintendents chat

#AussieEd – Australia education

#COLchat – Culture of learning

#digilead – Digital leadership

#EdBeat – For all teachers

#Edtechchat – Technology in education

#EDTherapy – Educational therapy

#FF – Follow Friday

#gtchat – Teachers of gifted students

#MSchat – Middle school teachers

#NJEd – New Jersey educators

#ntchat – New teachers chat

#PersonalizedPD – Professional development

#Satchat – Saturday chat

#SatchatME – Middle East Saturday chat

#SatchatOZ - Australia Saturday chat

#Satchathack – Saturday chat on holiday weekends

#SatchatWC – West Coast Saturday chat

#sschat – Social studies teachers

#stuvoice – Student voice

#Sunchat – Sunday chat

#tlap – *Teach Like a PIRATE*

#whatisschool – For all teachers

More From

Dave Burgess Consulting, Inc.

Teach Like a PIRATE

Increase Student Engagement, Boost Your Creativity, and Transform Your Life as an Educator

By Dave Burgess (@BurgessDave)

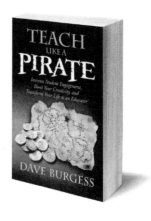

Teach Like a PIRATE is the *New York Times'* best-selling book that has sparked a worldwide educational revolution. It is part inspirational manifesto that ignites passion for the profession and part practical road map, filled with dynamic strategies to dramatically increase student engagement. Translated into multiple languages, its message resonates with educators who want to design outrageously creative lessons and transform school into a life-changing experience for students.

P is for PIRATE

Inspirational ABC's for Educators

By Dave and Shelley Burgess
(@Burgess_Shelley)

Teaching is an adventure that stretches the imagination and calls for creativity every day! In *P is for Pirate*, husband and wife team, Dave and Shelley Burgess, encourage and inspire educators to make their classrooms fun and exciting places to learn. Tapping into years of personal experience and drawing on the insights of more than seventy educators, the authors offer a wealth of ideas for making learning and teaching more fulfilling than ever before.

Ditch That Textbook

Free Your Teaching and Revolutionize Your Classroom
By Matt Miller (@jmattmiller)

Textbooks are symbols of centuries of old education. They're often outdated as soon as they hit students' desks. Acting "by the textbook" implies compliance and a lack of creativity. It's time to ditch those textbooks—and those textbook assumptions about learning! In *Ditch That Textbook*, teacher and blogger Matt Miller encourages educators to throw out meaningless, pedestrian teaching and learning practices. He empowers them to evolve and improve on old, standard teaching methods. *Ditch That Textbook* is a support system, toolbox, and manifesto to help educators free their teaching and revolutionize their classrooms.

Learn Like a PIRATE

Empower Your Students to Collaborate, Lead, and Succeed
By Paul Solarz (@PaulSolarz)

Today's job market demands that students be prepared to take responsibility for their lives and careers. We do them a disservice if we teach them how to earn passing grades without equipping them to take charge of their education. In *Learn Like a Pirate*, Paul Solarz explains how to design classroom experiences that encourage students to take risks and explore their passions in a stimulating, motivating, and supportive environment where improvement, rather than grades, is the focus. Discover how student-led classrooms help students thrive and develop into self-directed, confident citizens who are capable of making smart, responsible decisions, all on their own.

Pure Genius

Building a Culture of Innovation and
Taking 20% Time to the Next Level
By Don Wettrick (@DonWettrick)

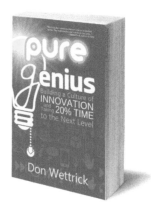

For far too long, schools have been bastions of boredom, killers of creativity, and way too comfortable with compliance and conformity. In *Pure Genius*, Don Wettrick explains how collaboration—with experts, students, and other educators—can help you create interesting, and even life-changing, opportunities for learning. Wettrick's book inspires and equips educators with a systematic blueprint for teaching innovation in any school.

The Innovator's Mindset

Empower Learning, Unleash Talent, and Lead a Culture of Creativity
By George Couros (@gcouros)

The traditional system of education requires students to hold their questions and compliantly stick to the scheduled curriculum. But our job as educators is to provide new and better opportunities for our students. It's time to recognize that compliance doesn't foster innovation, encourage critical thinking, or inspire creativity—and those are the skills our students need to succeed. In *The Innovator's Mindset*, George Couros encourages teachers and administrators to empower their learners to wonder, to explore—and to become forward-thinking leaders.

The Zen Teacher

Creating FOCUS, SIMPLICITY, and TRANQUILITY in the Classroom
By Dan Tricarico (@TheZenTeacher)

Teachers have incredible power to influence, even improve, the future. In *The Zen Teacher,* educator, blogger, and speaker Dan Tricarico provides practical, easy-to-use techniques to help teachers be their best—unrushed and fully focused—so they can maximize their performance and improve their quality of life. In this introductory guide, Dan Tricarico explains what it means to develop a Zen practice—something that has nothing to do with religion and everything to do with your ability to thrive in the classroom.

Master the Media

How Teaching Media Literacy Can Save Our Plugged-in World
By Julie Smith (@julnilsmith)

Written to help teachers and parents educate the next generation, *Master the Media* explains the history, purpose, and messages behind the media. The point isn't to get kids to unplug; it's to help them make informed choices, understand the difference between truth and lies, and discern perception from reality. Critical thinking leads to smarter decisions—and it's why media literacy can save the world.

50 Things You Can Do with Google Classroom

By Alice Keeler and Libbi Miller

(@AliceKeeler, @MillerLibbi)

It can be challenging to add new technology to the classroom, but it's a must if students are going to be well-equipped for the future. Alice Keeler and Libbi Miller shorten the learning curve by providing a thorough overview of the Google Classroom App. Part of Google Apps for Education (GAfE), Google Classroom was specifically designed to help teachers save time by streamlining the process of going digital. Complete with screenshots, *50 Things You Can Do with Google Classroom* provides ideas and step-by-step instructions to help teachers implement this powerful tool.

Your School Rocks...So Tell People!

*Passionately Pitch and Promote the Positives
Happening on Your Campus*

By Ryan McLane and Eric Lowe

(@McLane_Ryan, @EricLowe21)

Great things are happening in your school every day. The problem is: no one beyond your school walls knows about them. School principals Ryan McLane and Eric Lowe want to help you get the word out! In *Your School Rocks...So Tell People!,* McLane and Lowe offer more than seventy immediately actionable tips along with easy-to-follow instructions and links to video tutorials. This practical guide will equip you to create an effective and manageable communication strategy using social media tools. Learn how to keep your students' families and community connected, informed, and excited about what's going on in your school.

Play Like a Pirate

Engage Students with Toys, Games, and Comics

by Quinn Rollins

Yes! School can be simultaneously fun and educational. In *Play Like a Pirate*, Quinn Rollins offers practical, engaging strategies and resources that make it easy to integrate fun into your curriculum. Regardless of the grade level you teach, you'll find inspiration and ideas that will help you engage your students in unforgettable ways.

eXPlore Like a Pirate

*Gamification and Game-Inspired Course Design to
Engage, Enrich, and Elevate Your Learners*

By Michael Matera (@MrMatera)

Are you ready to transform your classroom into an experiential world that flourishes on collaboration and creativity? Then set sail with classroom game designer and educator, Michael Matera, as he reveals the possibilities and power of game-based learning. In *eXPlore Like a Pirate,* Matera serves as your experienced guide to help you apply the most motivational techniques of gameplay to your classroom. You'll learn gamification strategies that will work with and enhance (rather than replace) your current curriculum and discover how these engaging methods can be applied to any grade level or subject.

How Much Water Do We Have?

*5 Success Principles for Conquering Any Change and
Thriving in Times of Change*

by Pete Nunweiler with Kris Nunweiler

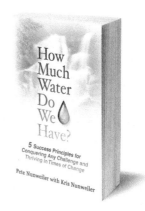

In *How Much Water Do We Have?* Pete Nunweiler identifies five key elements—information, planning, motivation, support, and leadership—that are necessary for the success of any goal, life transition, or challenge. Referring to these elements as the 5 Waters of Success, Pete explains that like the water we drink, you need them to thrive in today's rapidly paced world. If you're feeling stressed out, overwhelmed, or uncertain at work or at home, pause and look for the signs of dehydration. *How Much Water Do We Have?* will help you find, acquire, and use the 5 Waters of Success—so you can share them with your team and family members.

Brad Currie (@bradmcurrie) is the supervisor of instruction and dean of students for the Chester School District in Chester, New Jersey. He is also the founding partner and chief information officer for Evolving Educators, LLC.

Brad began his career in 2001 as a middle school social studies and computer education teacher for the Hanover Township School District in Whippany, New Jersey. He is a 2014 ASCD Emerging Leader, Google Certified Educator, Google Education Trainer, author of *All Hands on Deck: Tools for Connecting Parents, Educators, and Communities* and co-author of *Personalized PD: Flipping Your Professional Development*. He has been a featured blogger on *Edutopia*, penned a research-based article for the *Kappa Delta Pi Record*, and curated resources for a white paper on STEM leadership. Brad co-founded an online Twitter discussion for current and emerging school leaders called #Satchat.

Brad is married to a special education teacher, Leigh, and has two children, Cooper and Sydney. Learn more about Brad by following him on Twitter or visiting BradCurrie.net.

Billy Krakower (@wkrakower) is passionate about helping every child and adult enjoy and learn using technology tools in easy, fun, and empowering ways. He is the author of *Connecting Your Students with The World: Tools and Projects to Make Global Collaboration Come Alive, K-8* and *Using Technology to Engage Students with Disabilities*. Billy is part of ASCD's 2014 Emerging Leaders Class, a Google Educator, and a Microsoft Office Specialist. Billy is one of the lead organizers of EdCampNJ and EdCamp Leadership North New Jersey. He is on the teacher advisory board for ReadWorks. Billy is a member of the NJASCD

Executive Board, and he serves as the technology committee chair. He also served as co-director of NJASCD Northern Region (Fall 2013–June 2015). He has presented at more than twenty local and national technology conferences on topics including "Twitter & You," "The Science Behind a Mystery Location Call," and "Connecting Beyond the Classroom."

Billy has an advanced certificate in educational leadership and a dual master's degree in special education and elementary education from Long Island University. He is currently attending NYIT for his certificate in STEM education. You can read more about Billy at BillyKrakower.com.

Scott Rocco, Ed.D. (@ScottRRocco) is a super-intendent in Spotswood Public Schools in New Jersey, adjunct professor at The College of New Jersey, instructor in the NJEXCEL program, co-founder/co-moderator of #Satchat on Twitter, an EdCampNJ organizer, presenter, and keynote speaker. Before becoming superintendent, Scott was an assistant superintendent for human resources, an elementary school principal, middle school vice principal, and a high school and middle school social studies teacher.

Scott presents at local and state professional development trainings and conferences on the use of social media for educators, school safety, marketing yourself, and various leadership topics. He recently gave the closing keynote address at the Alaska Principals Association State Conference. Scott is dedicated to positively and productively engaging educators in a dialogue that improves student learning, enhances instruction, and creates effective learning environments for all who attend and work in schools. Follow Scott on Twitter and on his blog at EvolvingEducators.com.

CPSIA information can be obtained
at www.ICGtesting.com
Printed in the USA
BVOW10s1052270316

441905BV00006B/8/P